GARDENING WITH

ornamental
grasses

GARDENING WITH

ornamental grasses

ROGER GROUNDS

HORTICULTURE
BOOKS
www.hortmag.com

A HORTICULTURE BOOK

Horticulture Publications, Boston, Massachusetts

First published in the US in 2004   ISBN 1-55870-734-4

Reprinted 2004

Text © 2004 Roger Grounds

Horticulture is a subsidiary of F+W Publications Inc. Company
Distributed by F+W Publications Inc.
4700 East Galbraith Road, Cincinnati, OH 45236
1-800-289-0963

Printed in China by SNP Leefung
for Horticulture Publications, Boston, Massachusetts

Visit our website at www.hortmag.com

Some of the material in this book has appeared previously in
The Plantfinder's Guide to Ornamental Grasses by Roger Grounds.

PICTURE ACKNOWLEDGMENTS

Photos by Roger Grounds and Marie O'Hara except pp114 Jo Weeks
and pp100 and pp102 © Garden Picture Library
Illustrations by Coral Mula
Planting plans by Ethan Danielson

NOTE: Throughout the book the time of year is given as a season to make
the reference applicable to readers all over the world. In the northern hemisphere
the seasons may be translated into months as follows:

Early winter	December	*Early spring*	March	*Early summer*	June	*Early autumn*	September
Midwinter	January	*Mid-spring*	April	*Midsummer*	July	*Mid-autumn*	October
Late winter	February	*Late spring*	May	*Late summer*	August	*Late autumn*	November

CONTENTS

Why Grasses ?

The ideal garden plant is attractive in leaf, enchanting in flower, produces showy, long-lasting seedheads, often takes on glowing autumn colours, looks good for as much as half the year and is, moreover, easy to grow. Such are grasses. No other perennials offer so much interest over such a long season or contribute so much to setting the style and tone of a garden.

The magical thing about grasses is their intimacy with the natural world, the way they reflect its every mood – catching the sunlight in their flowers and seedheads or holding the morning dew suspended, changing with the passing hours, ebbing and flowing with the seasons, burgeoning in spring, maturing in summer, burning with tints of autumn fire and then becoming mere spectral shapes against the watery winter sun. Spangled with raindrops or rimed with frost, they have a poise and presence surpassed by no other plant.

Grasses come in all shapes and sizes, from little tussocks no higher than one's ankles to clumps as big as a lilac tree. They vary in shape from rounded mounds to stiffly upright or fountain-like clumps, while a few are carpeters. A few run at the roots, which can be useful (but they can also be avoided, if this is not desirable). Most thrive in ordinary garden earth and need no special fussing.

Beautiful though they are when grown alone, the greatest virtues of grasses become apparent only when they are combined with other plants.

What is a Grass?

Gardeners use the term 'grasses' loosely to embrace not only the true grasses but also several other plant groups that look like grasses, including sedges, rushes, cat-tails and a few lesser-known types. You don't need to be a botanist to enjoy growing ornamental grasses, but it does help if you know which are which, and something about the different kinds, their basic characteristics and their particular garden merits.

True grasses, Poaceae (or Gramineae), is a huge family containing not only lawn grasses and ornamental grasses but also those that produce our cereals, our bread, our confections and even our whisky. Their leaves are always flat with parallel veins and their stems are always round and hollow, a combination of characteristics not found in any other grass-like group. The stems have joints, called nodes, and the leaf sheaths are wrapped round the stems and can easily be pulled away. The roots are always fibrous. True grasses are mostly plants of poor soils and of open sunny places.

Sedges belong in the family Cyperaceae. Their stems are solid and triangular in section, and their leaves are strongly V-shaped. The old saw is 'sedges have edges' – the edges are the angles of the stems and leaves, which can be felt between finger and thumb. The leaf sheaths completely surround the stem and are difficult to pull away. The parts of the flowers are all in threes. The roots are always rhizomatous. Sedges tend to grow in damper and/or shadier places than the true grasses.

Rushes belong in the Junceae and have round stems like the true grasses but these are solid and do not have nodes (joints). All their leaves arise from ground level, and they do not have any leaves on their stems as the true grasses do. The flowers appear two-thirds of the way up the stem and are carried in flattened heads. Rushes are plants of moist, often ill-drained ground, and of the water's edge.

Cat-tails belong in the Typhaceae family. They are plants that grow in wet ground, such as that found at the edges of ponds and rivers, with their roots under water. They have strap-like leaves in two ranks and strongly spreading rhizomatous roots. The flowers are carried at the tops of round but solid stems; the fleeting male flowers are at the very tips, above the female flowers which are packed into what looks like a dark brown cigar.

Restios belong to the Restionaceae family and are a group of rush-like plants that are often well branched. The branches form whorls around the main stems. The flowers are small and brown and are produced at the tips of the main stems. Restios are plants of poor soils and will not grow well in enriched garden soil. Those that are in cultivation are mainly from South Africa.

Bamboos are true grasses from the Poaceae family but differ from other grasses in having woody stems that have branches and in that their leaves have stalks. They do not flower annually, like normal grasses, but at irregular intervals often many years apart. Then they flower massively, every shoot producing flowers and seeds. Most look dead after flowering, but will generally recover after a few years. One or two bamboos almost always have just a few flowers on them.

Grass-like plants is a vague term that embraces almost any kind of plant with long, narrow, 'grassy' leaves.

Flower forms

Most of the plants we grow in our gardens have big showy flowers with highly coloured petals. These are necessary to attract the birds and bees that pollinate them. Grasses are entirely different. They are wind-pollinated and the last thing they need is big showy petals getting in the way of the wind. Instead, the grasses produce large numbers of tiny flowers, each made up of little more than the essential reproductive organs, together with some bract-like structures that prevent self-pollination.

Calamagrostis brachytricha is typical of upright-divergent plant form.

The individual flowers are called spikelets and the spikelets are gathered together into flowerheads, called panicles, which can differ considerably in their shape and form. The simplest panicles are spikes and the spikelets are attached directly to a single, central axis. A raceme is similar but the individual spikelets are attached to the central axis by short stems. A panicle, in the strictest sense, has many side branches off the main axis, each of which behaves like a spike or a raceme.

Several grasses enhance their beauty by the addition of an awn. Awns are long, normally unbranched hair-like structures which arise from the part of the flower that turns into a seed, and they extend well beyond the flower. In a few grasses the awns are branched and feather-like and may be as much as 20cm (8in) long.

Stipa tenuissima has long awns that catch and hold the light from the sky.

Plant forms

Grasses can be divided into clumpers or runners. Most are clumpers and make tight, clumping plants, that can vary considerably in shape; some make rounded mounds, some grow narrowly upright, or arch outwards like a fountain under the weight of their flowers, some are upright-divergent, erect, narrow at the base, wider at the top, while a few are just plain floppy. There are also several grasses that have a running habit, which can be useful when you want to cover a large area, but can be a nuisance if you don't. Runners can, of course, be controlled, either with physical barriers or by frequent cultivation. In this book all the grasses mentioned are clumpers unless they are specifically stated to be runners.

A very few grasses can become a problem because they self seed excessively in some climates. The black-seeded fountain grasses, *Pennisetum alopecuroides* f. *viridescens* and *P. alopecuroides* 'Moudry', are examples, though in cool climates they can scarcely be induced to flower at all.

Grasses to be used with care

Below are some commonly troublesome grasses. However, it is difficult to be comprehensive since much depends on soil and climate. Some grasses – *Phragmites australis*, for example – can behave like clumpers when grown in ordinary earth but become rampant in wet ground or in a warmer climate.

Cortaderia jubata Showy pampas grass for warm climates. Can seed too freely.

Equisetum **species (scouring rushes)** Attractive primitive plants with leafless stems that can spread rampantly in ponds or wet ground.

Glyceria maxima **'Variegata' (striped manna grass)** Highly ornamental grasses with cream-and-green striped leaves, lovely at the waterside but will spread rampantly. Less spreading in ordinary earth.

Pennisetum alopecuroides **'Moudry',** *P. alopecuroides* f. *viridescens* Both may seed too freely in warm climates.

Phalaris arundinacea **and forms (gardener's garters, striped ribbon grass)** Very decorative with cream-, pink- or white-striped leaves, but spread persistently in most soils.

Phyllostachys aurea **and forms** Clump in cool climates, run in warm ones.

Phyllostachys nigra Clumps in cool climates, runs in warm ones.

Phragmites australis **and forms** Run slowly in ordinary earth, rampantly in wet soil or ponds.

Pleioblastus Most run strongly in all climates.

Sasa All run rampantly in most conditions.

Typha **(cat-tails)** All rampantly invasive in damp or wet ground in all climates.

Typha minima, the least invasive of the cat-tails.

Phalaris arundinacea 'Picta', a running grass whose spread needs to be contained or controlled.

Combinations

When combining grasses with other grasses or with other plants, it is important to match vigour with vigour. If a vigorous plant is put next to one that is more restrained in its growth, the more vigorous of the two will soon swamp the other. When the vigour is well matched, they will balance each other out, both flourishing without overwhelming each other. Where this sort of balance is achieved, the plants will use up the available moisture and nutrients, leaving little over for any weeds to enjoy. Of course, successful combinations are achieved partly through experience but balanced communities can be developed through trial and error and being prepared to move the plants around during the appropriate season.

What season?

Warm season

Most of the grasses we grow in our gardens flower after midsummer. They are known as warm-season grasses, because they wait until the warmth of summer before starting into growth, then grow rapidly and come into flower between mid- and late summer, the flowers turning quickly to seedheads, which then generally remain showy on the plants for many months. They are normally planted where they can fill the ground once spring-flowering bulbs or perennials are past their best. In cool climates it is usually disastrous to transplant or divide these grasses until they have started into growth.

Right: *Carex comans*, like most sedges, is usually treated as a cool season grower.

Below: *Imperata cylindrica* 'Rubra' with *Pennisetum alopecuroides* 'Woodside' – both are warm season growers.

Cool season

The remaining grasses are known as cool-season grasses, because they start into growth and flower while the weather is still cool, in spring and early summer, and tend to go into summer dormancy as temperatures rise. They are generally best planted, not at the front of a bed or border, but a little further back where other plants and grasses can grow up and hide them while they are dormant. Usually, they look better in summer if grown in woodland or a cool, shaded part of the garden. Cool-season grasses can be planted, transplanted and divided at almost any time, except when dormant in the heat of summer.

The distinction between the two types is important, both for how they are used in gardens and for how they are propagated. The main cool- and warm-season grasses are listed opposite. Additionally the seasonal status of each grass is noted in the A–Z of Grasses (pages 21–85).

Warm-season grasses

Andropogon all
Arundo all
Bouteloua curtipendula, B. gracilis
Chasmanthium latifolium
Chionochloa all
Chrysopogon gryllus
Cortaderia all
Elymus all
Erianthus all
Hystrix patula
Imperata cylindrica and forms
Miscanthus all
Molinia all
Panicum virgatum forms
Pennisetum all
Saccharum all
Schizachyrium scoparium
Sorghastrum nutans and forms
Spartina pectinata 'Aureomarginata'
Sporobolus heterolepis

Cool-season grasses

Arrhenatherum elatius subsp.
   bulbosum 'Variegatum'
Briza media
Calamagrostis x acutiflora forms
Carex species
Dactylis glomerata
Deschampsia cespitosa, D. flexuosa
Festuca all
Hakonechloa macra forms
Helictotrichon all
Holcus mollis and forms
Hystrix patula
Melica all
Milium effusum
Panicum 'Wood's Variegated'
Phalaris arundinacea forms
Poa all
Stipa most
Spodiopogon Because this flowers
   late some authorities place it among
   the warm-season growers.

The miscanthus at the top of the picture are typical warm season growers as is the panicum in the left corner and are in full flower in late summer while *Stipa tenuissima* (bottom right) is a cool season grower, its flowers long past.

Buying grasses

Always buy from a well-respected nursery or garden centre, where you can be confident that the plants are correctly named, and preferably from a nursery specializing in ornamental grasses. The best option is always to inspect the grasses in the nursery, but less usual varieties may only be obtainable by mail order.

Most grasses are sold in plastic pots but the sizes of the pots can vary from scarcely large enough to take a rooted offset to large enough to create mature plantings. In general, smaller plants establish more quickly than larger ones, though tiny ones often struggle. Always make sure that the top growth is turgid (not limp) and a good colour. Avoid grasses whose leaves are rolled. The leaves should be flat. Grasses roll their leaves when they are dry at the roots, and they may never recover from such dryness. Always turn the plant out of its pot. A healthy specimen

will have furry white roots running around the outside of the rootball, and there should be sufficient roots to hold the rootball together. If the soil falls away, this indicates that the plant has been recently repotted and it may be slow to establish. If the only visible roots are brown and matted, the plant has been in its pot too long and will be reluctant to establish in the garden. Avoid cheap plants: there is usually a reason why they are cheap. They are often of poor quality and are unlikely to mature into good plants.

Make sure the plant is what you want, that it is a suitable size and that it will grow well in your sort of soil, your climate and in the conditions found in the part of the garden you intend to plant it. You should find all the plant's requirements on the label, but if in doubt seek advice from the nursery or garden centre staff.

A feast of coloured foliage. *Imperata cylindrica* 'Rubra' with golden Hakone grass, *Hakonechloa macra* 'Alboaurea' to its left and a blue fecue, *Festuca glauca* to its right with *Molinia caerulea* 'Variegata' on the right.

Placing grasses

It is often prudent to place grasses (and indeed other sorts of plants) still in their pots where you think you want to plant them and then consider their placing for a day or two (or longer) before finally planting them. There are several factors to consider when choosing a grass for a particular spot.

The most important point is to choose the right plant for the right place. Is the garden habitat suitable for the plant you want to grow? Most grasses come from wide open spaces that have sunlight from dawn till dusk; plainly these will not do well in shaded places. They also come from poor soils and will grow out of character in richer soils. However, there are grasses that come from woodland margins and are suitable for more shaded positions, and some from wetter or richer soils. Sedges grow in damper and/or shadier places than the true grasses and they are often much more useful under shrubs and trees than the true grasses. Very damp or boggy soils are best suited to rushes of various sorts, though several of the sedges will also grow in boggy conditions. For the water's edge, the cat-tails are unsurpassed, though care must be taken to suit the vigour of the cat-tail to the size of the pond.

In general the flowers of grasses are displayed most effectively when the sun is beyond or beside them and they are against a dark background. The delicate structures of grass flowers capture sunlight in much the same way that water from a fountain captures it in its frothing bubbles. The same is true of grasses with variegated leaves. Having the sunlight beyond or beside them brings them to life in a way that they never achieve when the light is falling on them.

Top: The white foliage of *Miscanthus sinensis* 'Dixieland' contributes white to this white garden for far longer than the flowers of the *Phlox paniculata* 'David' next to it.

Centre: The yellow trumpets of *Digitalis grandiflora* echo the yellow bands on the leaves of *Miscanthus sinensis* 'Strictus'.

Below: The effulgence of the evening sun turns to gold the heavy, drooping panicles of *Ampelodesmos mauritanica* carefully sited to be seen against a dark background.

Caring for Grasses

One of the great virtues of grasses is that they demand little more than ordinary soil, a place in the sun and sufficient watering to get them established. The sedges prefer a damper soil than the true grasses, and will stand shade rather better, while the rushes and cat-tails can take a lot more moisture and will even be happy with their feet in water. While most grasses will grow well on most soils, some are more tolerant of extreme soils than others. (See pages 116–121 for grasses that can be grown on sandy soils, clays and so on. Grasses that are listed as doing well on these soils will, of course, grow well on most other soils.) Grasses are generally indifferent to the acidity or alkalinity of soils, but a few do have specific likes and dislikes (see page 118).

The preparation of the ground before planting will not present any problems. Where an extensive planting of grasses and companion plants is to be made, dig it over thoroughly and break down the sods. For specimen grasses, such as pampas grass or miscanthus, dig a hole 90cm (3ft) across and 45cm (18in) deep, then return the soil to it and make it firm before planting. Ideally, this preparatory work, which loosens the soil and allows freer movement of air and water and hence greater root penetration, should be done six months before planting to allow the ground to settle again.

Top: The worst weeds of large plantings of grasses are unwanted grasses.

Above: In mixed borders like this the grasses will need dividing far less frequently than the other elements.

Limitations of climate

The greatest single limiting factor in the growth of plants is the frequency of frosts. The map on page 126 shows the relative frequency of frosts in different defined zones of the US and these zone ratings are included in the A–Z of Grasses (pages 21–85). The figure given denotes the coldest zone in which the plant will flourish. Most will grow happily in warmer zones.

Feeding and watering

As a rule of thumb, grasses should be fed lightly or not at all; overfeeding makes them grow out of character and renders them prone to attack by pests and to problems with diseases. Most general-purpose fertilizers are suitable for light feeding, and it is usually most convenient to apply whatever you are using on the other plants in the garden, but at only a quarter of the rate. For the largest specimen grasses, miscanthus and pampas grass, some organic manure may be incorporated into the planting hole, and the same material used as a mulch in subsequent years.

While most grasses need watering during their first year to help them establish, the majority should be well able to withstand drought thereafter. Drought is, nonetheless, a stress for most grasses, and they generally look better if such stress can be avoided. Mulching is a method of moisture conservation to which they seem to respond particularly well. The best materials are organic substances such as processed bark, which is low in nutrient value, or fine gravel or pea-grit, which will gradually work into the soil, improving drainage and aeration.

The sedges and rushes, preferring damper ground, are rather heavier feeders than true grasses. As with the grasses, it is usually simplest to apply whatever fertilizer is being used in the rest of the garden, but this time at the same rate. They can also take heavier mulching with more nutrient-rich materials, such as garden compost. In times of drought most sedges, if well established, can be left to cope on their own. The leaves may wither and look rather wretched, but once rain returns they will recover.

Being gross feeders, bamboos are quite different in their needs from the generality of grasses. At planting time the prepared hole should be lavishly enriched with organic manure, and after planting the bamboo should be heavily mulched with a doughnut-like ring of manure. It should subsequently be fed with a general fertilizer as used in the rest of the garden, applied at the same rate. A yearly mulch of manure will be beneficial, not only for its nutrient value but also because of the moisture it conserves – important for bamboos, which also need to be grown in positions sheltered from winds for reasons of moisture conservation.

Bamboos are gross feeders and perform best when heavily fed and well mulched with organic materials.

Containment

Most grasses form clumps that increase in girth slowly but steadily so that in time they may become too large for their space. In this case, all that can be done is to dig up the grass, break it down into smaller pieces with a spade and put one of these pieces back. For those grasses that run at the roots a different approach is required. Sadly, people often avoid planting these grasses for fear that they will take over. However, all that is needed is to cut the roots back with a spade to the desired circumference, and then to fork out any runners outside that area. The rule is little and often; if this is done two or three times a year, the spread of the grasses can easily be controlled. It is when the grasses are left untended for a year or two that problems arise.

Right: This *Pleioblastus fortunei* has outgrown its pot and needs to be cut down and fertilized to restore its vigour

Below: *Phyllostachys vivax* 'Aureocaulis' needs a position sheltered from winds yet open to enough sun to bring out the rich colouring of the canes

Not all bamboos run, but those that do, such as the popular pleioblastus and phyllostachys, can be contained within a physical underground barrier. The taller the bamboo, the deeper the barrier should be – a minimum of 30cm (12in) for the smaller species and 75cm (30in) for the larger ones. Scrape away the earth from the top of the barrier once a year, and cut back any runners that are trying to escape over it. In the open ground, the spread of large bamboos, such as phyllostachys, can be controlled surprisingly easily, as long as the new shoots are dealt with during the growing season, which only lasts for a few weeks in spring and early summer. At this time, the shoots are soft and easily cut off below ground with a sharp spade or freezer knife. Go all round each bamboo in the growing season to ensure that all the runners have been removed. Smaller bamboos, such as pleioblastus, grow throughout the summer and are best contained.

Care

The only regular attention needed by most grasses is an annual grooming, and this is best done at the end of winter. For deciduous grasses that have lost all the colour in their leaves, cut the stems down close to the ground – the smaller ones to within 1–2.5cm (1–2in), the larger ones, such as miscanthus, to 12.5–15cm (5–6in). Evergreen grasses, those that retain colour in a high proportion of their leaves, should not be cut down but merely trimmed over lightly to remove the scorched tips of the leaves. Rake out dead leaves and debris with the fingers or with a small garden fork.

It is usually as well to tidy the ground around the plants at the same time, and to apply any mulches or fertilizers. The grasses can then be left to ebb and flow through another season with little further intervention. Indeed, in most gardens the biggest problem with ornamental grasses is that weed grasses may seed themselves into the crowns of desirable species. It is important to keep on top of this and not allow the weeds to become established.

At the end of winter cut down grasses that turn biscuit coloured like this *Phalaris arundinacea* 'Picta' but leave evergreen grasses well alone

Propagation

The propagation of grasses (including sedges and rushes) is, on the whole, straightforward. All species and their botanical varieties, including the annuals, can be raised from seed, and variegated grasses will produce about 20 per cent variegated seedlings. If seed cannot be sown at once it should be stored. A common practice is to keep it in envelopes in an airtight container in a garage or frost-free outhouse, though the seed of most cool-season grasses needs three weeks chilling in a refrigerator before it will germinate. Seed can be sown in spring or early summer, either in a coldframe or out of doors where it is to grow. If grown under glass, the seedlings should be well ventilated to prevent damping off. They are liable to the usual pests and problems of any young seedlings, including damage by slugs and snails.

Named varieties of grasses must be increased by division, cool-season growers in spring or autumn (never in summer), warm-season growers only in the spring or early summer. When dividing grasses that are in full leaf, cut back the foliage to a quarter of its length.

The easiest way to divide a grass is to dig up the whole plant and then to break it into smaller pieces. With small grasses, such as milium, this can easily be done by hand, but with large grasses, such as miscanthus, more force is needed – some have such tough roots that it is necessary to use an axe or a saw. Some grasses, such as the cushion-forming fescues, can be divided into single bundles of leaves with roots, but most of the larger species, *Pennisetum alopecuroides* and miscanthus for example, should never be divided down to the smallest possible pieces. Grasses that produce runners, such as *Phalaris arundinacea*, can be propagated by detaching pieces that have rooted and growing them on, either in pots or in the open ground.

One or two grasses can be increased by stem or root cuttings – indeed, cuttings are the usual means of increasing *Arundo donax* and *A. d.* 'Variegata'. The technique is to remove sideshoots with a short length of old stem attached, and to lay them obliquely in a shallow pan of water. They will usually send out roots in a matter of days, and can be potted on once they have sufficient. Best results are usually obtained in early summer.

Cuttings of sections of the canes of *Saccharum officinarum* (sugar cane) will root at the nodes if laid on their sides in potting mix: take the cuttings between the nodes, so that each cutting contains at least one node.

Grow on newly propagated grasses in a position sheltered from wind, and if propagated in summer, also provide protection from hot sun – drying out is the greatest danger to young grasses. Attention should be paid to watering; no amount of overwatering later will ever make up for momentary desiccation. Beware of frosts, too: young grasses are often more vulnerable to frost than they will be once established, and this is particularly true of miscanthus.

Far left: Timing is crucial to success in propagating grasses. Warm season growers, like the miscanthus (top left and extreme right) and the panicum (top right) need to be divided in late spring or early summer, once they have started into growth, while cool season growers, like the *Stipa tenuissima* (lower left) can be divided almost any time provided there is neither drought nor frost.

Pests and diseases

Grasses are remarkably untroubled by pests and diseases. Though one or two common garden pests may be a nuisance, foliar rust is the only disease that can be a problem, and that only with some grasses. It is a fungal disease revealing itself as small, rusty-orange nodules or spots on the leaves. The only real treatment is to apply wettable sulphur several times through the season, beginning before susceptible grasses start into growth. Apply the sulphur to the ground around the grasses, not to the grasses themselves. Increased air circulation around the plants reduces the likelihood of rust, too.

Blue lyme grass (*Leymus arenarius*) can suffer in some districts from the presence of stem smut fungus, *Ustilago hypodytes*, which prevents it from flowering properly. Instead it produces culms that are positively scrofulous with the black spore pustules. Since the fungus infests the tissues throughout the plant, the only remedy is to burn the entire thing.

Aphids sometimes attack the soft new growth of grasses, especially under glass or in tunnels, but the damage is usually not great; grasses grow so vigorously that they soon leave the damaged growth behind, and the aphids cannot keep up. They can be washed off the foliage with a jet of water, or suffocated with a spray of insecticidal soap.

Mealybugs are more serious. If these little white insects are around at all, they will be found down inside the sheaths, where they wrap around the soft part of the culm, which they eat. They can be destroyed by alcohol applied with a soft brush or cottonwool swabs.

Slugs and snails may damage some grasses, in particular sedges, though most grasses are never affected. Vulnerable plants are those with soft leaves, such as *Milium effusum* and *Carex siderosticha*, as well as some of the subtropical species. There is no absolute cure. Damage is best limited by hand-picking slugs and snails at night and placing them in a bucket of salt or soapy water. Slug pellets also achieve a measure of control, though most controls are increasingly seen as ecologically unsound. Strips consisting of copper and diatomaceous earth (Mol-bar) have a deterrent effect.

Rabbits can be a serious problem in some gardens, and regard some grasses, deschampsia in particular, as first-rate fodder, though they do not generally bother with grasses that have wiry leaves. Rabbit fencing is really the only effective strategy, though the cost of erecting such a barrier can be prohibitive.

Deer are not a serious problem with grasses, though they will sample anything that is newly planted and will sometimes browse on new growth. Generally they leave grasses alone once the leaves have hardened. Like rabbits, they tend to avoid grasses with tough or wiry leaves. Deer fencing is the ultimate deterrent. Some folk remedies, such as bags of human hair hung on fences, may be effective.

A–Z
of Grasses

The grasses in this chapter are my own choice
and represent those I consider worthy of a
place in the garden. I have given each a
rating out of ten: ten is best, one is worst.
Anything that scores less than five is probably
not worth growing.

Key

↕ Grasses: Height of the plant in flower
Bamboos: Height and width of the cane

↔ Grasses: How far apart to place plants
Bamboos: Dimensions of the clumps over years

✷ Flowering season

Z The coolest hardiness zone in the USA in which the plant can be grown (see page 126 for the zone map)*

❊/❊ For grasses, warm-season grower or cool-season grower**

*Not relevant for annuals.

**Not relevant for annuals, restios, rushes, sedges or grass-like plants.

AGM after the plant's name means that the plant has been given an Award of Garden Merit after trial by the Royal Horticultural Society.

Achnatherum see Stipa (page 82)

Acorus

Eurasia

Waterside or marginal grass-like plants with iris-like leaves and surface-creeping rhizomes, belonging to the arum family. The flowers consist of a small brownish spathe and spadix but are seldom noticed.

A. calamus

Sweet flag

Often mistaken for an iris from the size and shape of the leaves, this is included here for 'Argenteostriatus' ('Variegatus'), a form with strongly but neatly white-striped leaves, flushed red or pink in spring. The leaves emit a cinnamon scent when crushed; 9/10.

↕	90cm/36in
↔	30cm/12in
✺	late spring–early summer
Z	4

A. gramineus

Grass-like plant with fans of narrow green leaves arising from a surface-creeping rhizome; 5/10. 'Ogon' ('Wogon') has evenly golden-yellow leaves; 8/10. 'Oborozuki' has vibrant yellow leaves and is interesting planted as a carpet beneath yellow selections of *Phormium tenax* such as 'Radiance', 'Williamsii' or 'Yellow Queen' or *P. cookianum* 'Cream Delight' or 'Surfer'; 8/10. var. *pusillus* is a diminutive form with green leaves seldom more than 8cm (3in) high; 6/10. 'Variegatus' is commonly grown and has leaves striped cream and yellow; it makes an interesting carpet beneath *Phormium tenax* 'Variegata', which it imitates in miniature; 7/10. 'Yodo-no-yuki' has leaves striped dark and light green; 6/10. All forms suffer rust pustules on the leaves if too dry at the roots.

↕	20cm/8in
↔	20cm/8in
✺	late spring–early summer
Z	4

Agrostis

Mainly northern hemisphere

A genus of 120 or so of annual and perennial grasses.

A. canina

Velvet bent, brown bent

Perennial grass common in lawns. 'Silver Needles' is smaller than the green form and makes a dense carpet of thin, white-edged leaves topped in summer by foxy-red flowers. Clumps have a tendency to die out in the centre. This can be reduced but not eliminated by clipping the plants over with shears after flowering. Europe; 6/10.

↕	20cm/8in
↔	15cm/6in
✺	early–midsummer
Z	4–8
☀/☀	cool

A. nebulosa

Cloud grass

Annual grass with a huge diffuse flower panicle tipped with tiny spikelets creating a cloud-like effect. Enchanting in drifts at the front of the border and suitable for cutting; 8/10.

↕	35cm/14in
↔	15cm/6in
✺	late spring–midsummer

Aira Hair grass

Eurasia, especially round the Mediterranean

A genus of nine annual grasses with hair-like leaves and cloud-like panicles of tiny spikelets.

↕ 30cm/12in

↔ 15cm/6in

✳ late spring–midsummer

A. elegantissima AGM

Low-growing annual with open, pyramidal panicles composed of purple-tinted, hair-fine branches tipped with tiny, silvery grey spikelets. Decorative both in the garden and picked. Needs care if it is to be used as a dried decoration as the spikelets and branches easily become entangled and break when the bunch is pulled apart; 8/10.

Alopecurus Foxtail grass

Temperate northern hemisphere

A genus of 25 annual or perennial grasses.

↕ 30cm/12in

↔ 15cm/6in

✳ late spring–midsummer

Z 4–7

✂ cool

A. alpinus

Alpine foxtail grass

Perennial slowly forming loose mats of intensely silvery blue leaves, often tinged with purple, especially when young. Flowers similar in colour to the leaves. subsp. *glaucus* ('Glaucus') seems little different. Delightful at all seasons, needing only sun and good drainage. Both 8/10.

A. pratensis

Meadow foxtail

↕ 90cm/36in

↔ 60cm/24in

✳ mid-spring–early summer

Z 5

✂ cool

The typical green-leaved form is a plant of meadows scarcely worthy of the garden. **'Aureovariegatus'** ('Aureomarginata'), golden foxtail grass, is smaller than the typical form with leaves striped and edged golden yellow. In spring it is the brightest yellow of all grasses, though overtaken later in the season by *Hakonechloa macra* 'Aureola'. The flowers are reddish brown cylindrical foxtails rising a little above the foliage. Easy in most soils in sun; on poor soils it will make a diminutive plant – no more than 5–7.5cm (2–3in) tall with leaves no more than 7.5cm (3in) long – with a running habit, while on rich, loamy soils the leaves can reach 30cm (12in) but the plant then tends to form clumps rather than running. Where it adopts this clumping habit, which is most often on heavy clay, the clumps need to be lifted and divided every 2–3 years to maintain vigour, though on poor soils it can be left to run. The form **'Aureus'** has entirely yellow leaves. Best in sun in cool climates and in light shade in warm climates; 9/10.

Alopecurus pratensis
'Aureovariegatus'

Ampelodesmos

Mauritania
A genus of a single perennial grass. Grown for
the earliness of its showy flowers.

↕	2.75m/9ft
↔	90cm/36in
✳	late spring–midsummer
Z	8
⚘	warm

A. mauritanica

Mauritanian vine reed, Mauritanian rope grass
Large clumps of dark evergreen leaves and
slender arching stems of huge, heavy panicles of
chaffy buff spikelets, hanging in one-sided plumes.
Suitable for cutting. Needs a sunny, well-drained
position. Not reliably hardy in colder areas;
9/10.

Ampelodesmos mauritanica

Andropogon Beard grass

North America
A genus of 100 or so annual and perennial grasses. Those grown in gardens are
all deciduous, clump-forming perennials flowering in late summer. Most take on
rich autumnal tints and are good for cutting.

A. gerardii

Big bluestem, turkey foot
This has a strongly upright habit and produces many-fingered flowers which have a
fancied resemblance to the foot of a turkey. Does best in hot, dry sites on poor soils.
The powder-blue leaves are usually tipped and stained purple, the colouring intensifying
after midsummer, the whole plant turning a rich brown for winter; 7/10. **'Sentinel'** has
a narrow stiffly upright habit and is even bluer; 10/10. Both look good among greys
and silvers, and with the mauves of *Aster novi-belgii* varieties like 'Chequers', 'Coombe
Rosemary' and 'Royal Velvet' or the lighter tones of the long-flowering *A.* x *frikartii*
'Mönch' or 'Flora's Delight' as well as with the enlivening yellows of *Rudbeckia fulgida*
'Goldsturm'; the asters and rudbeckias are derived from natives of the same prairies.

↕	1.5m/5ft
↔	45cm/18in
✳	late summer–early autumn
Z	4
⚘	warm

↕	90cm/36in
↔	45cm/18in
✳	early–mid-autumn
Z	5
⚘	warm

A. glomeratus

Bushy beard grass
Grown more for its flowers than its greenish foliage, the flowers being produced in a
dense tuft, surrounded by clusters of bushy bracts at the tops of stiffly upright stems,
giving it a unique appearance. In autumn the whole plant turns rich burnt orange, this
colour lasting through winter. Needs long, hot summers to flower and to show its
autumn colouring. Not a success in Britain; 3/10.

↕	1.2m/4ft
↔	30cm/12in
✳	early–mid-autumn
Z	3
⚘	warm

A. virginicus

Broom sedge
Densely upright and clump-forming with green leaves and stems that gradually suffuse
with vinous purplish colouring which intensifies as flowering approaches. In autumn the
leaves turn bright orange-red, the colour lasting all winter. Flowers are small white
'beards' borne in clusters scattered along the stems in company with long, thin bracts.
Perfectly frost hardy but needs long hot summers to flower freely and colour well in
winter; 3/10.

Anemanthele

New Zealand

A single perennial grass that has previously been called *Stipa arundinacea* and *Oryzopsis rigida*.

↕	90cm/36in
↔	60cm/24in
❋	midsummer–early autumn
Z	7
✳⁄❋	warm

A. lessoniana

Gossamer grass, pheasant grass, wind grass

Loose clumps of long, narrow olive-green leaves, overlaid with rusty colours, in autumn becoming splashed and blotched with yellows, reds and oranges. Red-stemmed lax and diffuse panicles, bearing few spikelets, only just appear beyond the foliage. Best leaf colouring is obtained on plants growing in poor soils or starved in pots. Seeds itself around lightly in many gardens, and makes an excellent groundcover in sun or in light shade; 9/10.

Anthoxanthum

Eurasia and North America

A genus of five or six aromatic annual and perennial grasses.

↕	60cm/24in
↔	22cm/9in
❋	late spring–early summer
Z	7
✳⁄❋	cool

A. odoratum

Sweet vernal grass

Grown for the coumarin fragrance of its leaves, particularly strong when it is in flower, and when dried. A small, clumping evergreen grass with soft, mid-green leaves, the cylindrical, spike-like panicles being silky green at first becoming whitish. Not showy in flower; 5/10.

Arrhenatherum

Mediterranean region

A genus of six perennial grasses.

A. elatius subsp. bulbosum

Bulbous couch grass, bulbous oat grass

↕	30cm/12in
↔	15cm/6in
❋	mid-spring–early summer
Z	7
✳⁄❋	cool

The type is an obnoxious weed, spreading rapidly by means of bulbils produced at the nodes. 'Variegatum', striped bulbous couch grass, is quite the brightest of the white-variegated grasses, the rather soft, upright leaves being striped and conspicuously margined purest white. The flowers, by contrast, are miffy little off-white affairs of no ornamental merit. This cool season grower starts into growth in autumn and grows intermittently through winter. It goes into summer dormancy, often fading away completely until autumn. Plant it in shade to prolong its season of beauty, preferably in moist acid soils; it tends to languish on heavy clays. Best placed where summer-growing plants can spring up to hide its fading foliage. Divide frequently; 9/10.

Arundinaria see Fargesia (see page 46)

Arundo

Eurasia

Three species of strongly rhizomatous perennial grasses natives of wet ground and river banks.

A. donax

Provençal reed, giant reed

↕ 4.5m/15ft

↔ 90cm/36in

✽ early–mid-autumn

Z 7

❊ warm

The largest and most architectural of all frost-hardy perennial grasses. Thick glaucous grey-green stems arise from a stout rootstock and are upright at first, splaying outwards later; they have similarly coloured leaves arranged in two ranks and spaced at equal intervals up them. The flowers are as spectacular as the plant, being huge fluffy panicles as much as 60cm (2ft) long and 25cm (10in) across but seldom seen in cool climates. Attains its fullest development in warm sheltered gardens on rich, moist soils. Tends to clump in cool gardens and spread in warm gardens. Can make a stunning specimen or screen, and can help to create a subtropical ambience. As the season advances the stems branch and the leaves tend to split at the tips. Probably best cut to the ground every winter, though if flowers are wanted the culms should be left for a second year. Cuttings of sideshoots, taken in summer, root readily in wet sand; 9/10. 'Golden Chains' has gold-variegated leaves and reaches about 1.2m (4ft); 9/10. 'Macrophylla' has broader, thicker leaves, more glaucous than the type; 9/10. var. *versicolor* ('Variegata'), striped Provençal reed, striped giant reed, is probably the most stunning of all variegated grasses, the broad leaves are boldly striped white or creamy white, being whitest in cool conditions, creamiest in warm, almost fading to green after long, hot summers. Not so tall nor so hardy as the typical plant, excellent in conservatories; 10/10.

Avena Oats, Wild oats

Europe, Asia and parts of North Africa

A genus of about 15 annual grasses, related to *A. sativa*, the cultivated oat, which they resemble in general appearance.

A. sterilis

Animated oat, wild oat

↕ 90cm/36in

↔ 45cm/18in

✽ early–late summer

A loosely tufted annual producing light, open, widely branched, arching heads with nodding spikelets, green at first becoming straw-coloured and bearing a strong resemblance to the cultivated oat. One of the few annual grasses that seems to do better on heavy soils. Popular for picking and drying. Known as the animated oat because the long awns twist and writhe whenever the atmospheric humidity changes, especially when the panicles have been dried; 9/10.

Bouteloua

Argentina to Canada

About 30 annual and perennial grasses from dry grasslands. Sometimes confused with *Chondrosum*.

B. gracilis

Mosquito grass, blue grama

Dense mounds of finely textured grey-green foliage, the flowers borne well above them. The flowering stems, which are thin as wire, rise almost straight up out of the mound with the part that bears the flowers seemingly attached at a right angle to the main stem. The spikelets hang down beneath this axis like the larvae of mosquitoes hanging from the surface of water – hence the common name. The spikelets are silvery grey at first gradually growing darker, being almost purple at maturity. The whole plant assumes purplish autumnal colour before bleaching out for winter. Drought-tolerant once established; 7/10.

↕	30cm/12in
↔	30cm/12in
✿	late spring–late summer
Z	3
❋	warm

Briza Quaking grass

Temperate Eurasia and South America

A genus of 20 annual and perennial grasses.

B. maxima

Quaking grass, greater quaking grass

A popular annual with curious locket-shaped flowerheads composed of overlapping scales, reminiscent of the tip of a rattlesnake's tail, produced on a loosely tufted plant. An excellent foil to brightly coloured annuals and lovely for picking and drying; 8/10.

↕	30cm/12in
↔	15cm/6in
✿	late spring–early summer

Briza maxima

B. media

Quaking grass, common quaking grass, didder, dickies, doddering dillies

Quaint rather than beautiful, this perennial quaking grass forms loose tufts of thin, mid-green leaves and branching panicles bearing small, locket-like spikelets at the tips. The plant is green to start with but gradually takes on shades of biscuit, becoming dormant by midsummer. New leaves start into growth in autumn. 'Limouzi' is taller with bluer leaves and larger spikelets; 9/10.

↕	60cm/24in
↔	23cm/9in
✿	late spring–early summer
Z	5
❋	cool

Briza minor

B. minor

Lesser quaking grass

This is a miniature version of *B. maxima*, also annual and a little jewel. Thrives and self seeds in warm, sandy soils but can prove difficult on heavy soils; 8/10.

↕	23cm/9in
↔	10cm/4in
✿	late spring–early summer

Bromus Brome, brome grass

Temperate northern hemisphere
About 100 species of annual and perennial grasses.

↕	60cm/24in
↔	60cm/24in
❀	early–late summer
Z	5
✳	cool

B. inermis

Smooth brome

Perennial grass usually grown in the form **'Skinner's Gold'**, a fairly new and still unstable selection with leaves that are strikingly assymetrically striped gold and green. Above these are borne elegant open panicles of relatively large, drooping, corn-gold spikelets. Spreads gently at the roots and tends to make untidy clumps; 6/10.

↕	60cm/24in
↔	15cm/6in
❀	late spring–midsummer

B. madritensis

A loosely tufted annual producing showy panicles, about 15cm (6in) long, composed of coarse-bristled spikelets that look like bundles of small egg-whisks. It is one of the few annual grasses that will do well in some shade. The panicles shatter as soon as they are dried, even if picked before the flowers open; 5/10.

↕	1m/39in
↔	30cm/12in
❀	mid–late summer
Z	5
✳	cool

B. ramosus

Wood brome, hairy brome

Useful as a shade-tolerant grass, this differs from other shade-tolerant grasses in its greater height. It produces elegant, arching panicles of bristly spikelets in summer. Its one disadvantage is that it spreads freely by seed and so it is best confined to wilder parts of the garden; 5/10.

Calamagrostis Reed grass

Temperate northern hemisphere
About 250 perennial grasses, mostly natives of dampish places.

↕	1.8m/6ft
↔	1m/39in
❀	early–late summer
Z	5
✳	cool

C. x acutiflora

Feather reed grass

A naturally occurring hybrid most commonly grown in the form **'Karl Foerster'** ('Stricta'). This is one of the most valuable of ornamental grasses because from its coming up to its dying down it is the very paradigm of verticality, and, like anything vertical, draws the eye strongly. Also excellent for screening. It is a virtually sterile clumping grass that starts into growth rather earlier in the spring than other grasses, forming a tuft of narrow dark green leaves. The panicles start to emerge in late spring, slender as pipe cleaners atop shiny green stems that are straight as a ramrod, ultimately reaching some 1.5m (5ft) in height. In early summer the panicles relax, becoming loose and open and subtly tinted purple. Then, once flowering is over, the branches of the panicle close up against the main axis and the panicle again becomes as narrow as a pipe cleaner, gradually changing to a rich beige, which it remains all through the summer and autumn and into the winter. The stiff stems bend under the weight of rain or before the force of the wind, but never break, provided

Calamagrostis x *acutiflora*
'Karl Foerster'

Calamagrostis x acutiflora 'Overdam'

↕ 1.2m/4ft

↔ 3ft/90cm

✽ late summer–mid-autumn

Z 6

✳✿ warm

that it is grown in poor soil. In shade and in rich soils the stems become lax and prone to breaking under severe weather conditions. Also good for cutting; 10/10.
'Overdam', striped feather reed grass, is a sport with white-variegated foliage, the new leaves tinged pink. It is slightly shorter than the green-leaved form, otherwise similar; 9/10.

C. brachytricha (*Acnatherum brachytricha, Stipa brachytricha*)
Korean feather reed grass
Highly ornamental perennial grass easily grown in most soils in sun or a little shade, its foliage emerging early in the season, rich green often tinted bronzy purple, colouring that fades in the summer but returns in the autumn. Flower stems, almost formally upright-divergent, produce egg-shaped feathery panicles of pinkish grey. In

Calamagrostis brachytricha

warm-summer climates the habit is quite stiffly upright, but in cooler, damper climates it is more relaxed. The finest grass for late summer display and valuable in winter, the panicles remaining intact till early spring. Also suitable for cutting; 10/10.

Carex
Cool temperate regions worldwide
A large genus of mainly evergreen grass-like plants from damp or moist soil. Many are happy in shade and are especially valuable in shaded and woodland gardens.

C. albula
Blonde sedge

↕ 30cm/12in

↔ 30cm/12in

✽ late spring–early summer

Z 7

A distinctive and beautiful New Zealand sedge with an upright, tufted habit and almost thread-like leaves of such a pale green that they appear almost white, especially in the coldest months of the year. Flowers are insignificant. Easy in most soils in sun or slight shade, and relatively drought-tolerant once established. Seeds itself lightly in cool climates, the seedlings coming true to colour. Best planted in pots or on a ledge so that its cascading habit can be appreciated. Much confused in the trade with *C. comans* or *C. comans* 'Frosted Curls', which differs in its cascading, flowing habit and in the little curls at the tips of the leaves; 8/10.

C. buchananii AGM
New Zealand everbrown sedge

↕ 60cm/24in

↔ 60cm/24in

✽ late spring–early summer

Z 7

Probably the most popular of the red-leaved New Zealand sedges, this is upright when young but becomes more spreading with age, forming sprawling brown tussocks. The leaves are rolled and appear thread-like with the tips bleached and tightly curled. It colours best in sun and seeds itself around in the well-drained soils that suit it best. Withstands drought quite well once established; 8/10.

Carex buchananii

C. comans
New Zealand hair sedge

A densely tufted species, similar to *C. albula* in its thread-like foliage but differing in its typically cascading, flowing habit. In the wild the foliage varies from reds to browns to pale greens, but the tip of each leaf always has a distinctive little curl and is also bleached in sun. Flowering stems are about as long as the leaves but continue to extend after flowering so that seed is distributed around the edges of the plant, and may reach as much as 1.2m (4ft) long. Easy in most well-drained but

Carex comans

moisture-retentive soils in sun; 6/10. **'Bronze'** is an umbrella name for any of the reddish or brownish forms. In the best forms the new leaves are distinctly pinkish brown, the bases of the leaves green. Further selection is yielding named forms with cleaner colours, see 'Taranaki'. **'Frosted Curls'** has very pale green leaves which together with the bleached, curly tips, gives it an almost white appearance. It was found as a single plant in the wild by Terry Hatch of Joy Plants in Pukekohe, New Zealand, and all true plants have been derived vegetatively from that original plant. Some plants sold as 'Frosted Curls' are not true. The true plant has foliage that is soft to the touch. *C. albula* is sometimes sold as 'Frosted Curls' but differs in its more upright habit and in lacking the curling tips to the leaves; 10/10. **'Taranaki'** ('Small Red') is a selection from 'bronze'. It has good reddish foliage and reaches about 23cm (9in); 8/10. Sometimes confused with *C. flagellifera*, which is taller, more upright and lacks the little curls at the tips of the leaves.

C. conica 'Snowline'

A pleasing little sedge with narrow, arching, dark green leaves that have narrow white margins, and spikes of whitish flowers that stand just above the leaves. Not wintergreen. Easy in most soils; prefers it damper rather than drier. Slow to increase. 'Hime-kan-suge', sometimes used as a varietal name, is the Japanese name for this plant; 6/10.

C. dipsacea

A curious and distinctly upright New Zealand sedge whose channelled leaves vary from olive green to bright orange depending on the amount of sun or shade. Readily distinguished from *C. testacea* (which seed) by their almost black seedheads and in that they remain within the spread of the leaf mound; 5/10.

C. dolichostachya 'Kaga-Nishiki'

From Japanese mountain woodlands, this forms symmetrical fountain-like mounds of narrow green foliage strongly edged with gold, accompanied by small, whitish tufts of flowers. Colours best in sun but will tolerate a little shade. Prefers dampish soil but can tolerate drought once established. Sometimes sold as 'Gold' or 'Golden Fountain' or Fountains; 8/10.

↕ 30cm/12in
↔ 30cm/12in
❁ late spring–early summer
Z 7

↕ 15cm/6in
↔ 10cm/4in
❁ late spring–early summer
Z 7

↕ 45cm/18in
↔ 30cm/12in
❁ late spring–early summer
Z 7

↕ 25cm/10in
↔ 30cm/12in
❁ late spring–early summer
Z 6

↕	75cm/30in
↔	60cm/24in
✽	late spring–early summer
Z	5

C. elata 'Aurea' AGM
Bowles' golden sedge
This provides about the brightest gold-yellow in the garden in spring when the leaves first appear, and it maintains its colour well through the summer. The leaves are yellow with thin green margins; the forms **'Knightshayes'** AGM and **'Sue Ward'** lack the green edges. The black flowers are produced on arching stems in early summer but are soon overtaken by the foliage. Needs wet soil or the water's edge, especially when grown in sun, where the colouring is most intense; needs less moisture at the roots when grown in shade, though in shade the colouring is usually lime

Carex elata 'Sue Ward'

green. Scorches in hot-summer climates, even when not exposed to sun. Lovely with blue-flowered Siberian irises and pink or red astrantias, which enjoy the same conditions; 10/10.

↕	30cm/12in
↔	indefinite
✽	late spring–midsummer
Z	7

C. flacca (*C. glauca* misapplied)
Carnation grass
C. flacca forms carpets of narrow blue leaves with a superficial resemblance to those of carnations. Useful for its blueness but its running habit can be a problem. A good companion for flowers in shades of apricot or terracotta; 6/10. **'Bias'** is a selection with a white margin on one side of the leaf; 5/10.

↕	30cm/12in
↔	20cm/8in
✽	mid–late spring
Z	6

C. flaccosperma
Grown for the intense blue colouring of its wide pleated leaves, at their best in the summer, fading to a dull bluish-green in winter. The flowers and flower stems are the same colour as the leaves. Easily grown on most soils, better damp than dry though reasonably drought-tolerant; 6/10.

↕	45cm/18in
↔	30cm/12in
✽	late spring–midsummer
Z	7

C. flagellifera
As cultivated in Britain, this appears similar to *C. comans* 'bronze' but in the wild it can vary from green through dingy greyish bronze to quite clean reddish browns. It is generally taller and less spreading than *C. comans*, and prefers to be grown in rather damper soils. As with *C. comans* and *C. testacea*, the flowering stems continue to elongate after flowering and ultimately extend far beyond the leaf mound; 6/10.

Carex flagellifera

↕	35cm/14in
↔	60cm/24in
✿	late spring–midsummer
Z	7

↕	23cm/9in
↔	60cm/24in
✿	late spring–early summer
Z	6

↕	45cm/18in
↔	30cm/12in
✿	mid–late spring
Z	7

↕	60cm/24in
↔	30cm/12in
✿	early–midsummer
Z	7

↕	15cm/6in
↔	15cm/6in
✿	late spring–midsummer
Z	7

C. fraseri (*Cymophyllus fraseri*)
Fraser's sedge
A native of deep rich damp soils in woodlands in North America, this sedge is different from all others. It slowly forms expanding clumps of wide leaves, like those of a tulip but minutely toothed at the margins, which lie on the ground or are held only just above it. The flowers are small, clean white pompoms held well above the leaves. Needs rich moist soil and shade for most of the day. Will tolerate a dense deciduous canopy; 9/10.

C. glauca
The bluest of the evergreen North American sedges, its broad, somewhat pleated leaves are much the same electric blue as those of *Hosta* 'Halcyon' all year round. A clumper producing blue flowers on blue stems in early summer; 7/10.

C. morrowii
Morrow's sedge
Forms dense tufts of long straight evergreen leaves that seem to radiate out from the centre of the plant; 5/10. 'Variegata' is the best known of several variegated forms, its leaves margined and faintly striped white. Quite showy beige and cream flowers are borne just above the leaves. Tolerant of both damp and dry conditions, and shade or sun. 'Fisher's Form' is similar but larger in all its parts with cream variegation. In the USA the same plant is called 'Gold Band'. 'Gilt' is similar but smaller. All 8/10.

Two further varieties generally included here are quite different in their flowers and in their slowly running habit, making them useful groundcovers. *C.*'Silver Sceptre' has narrow arching leaves, variegated dull white. Scorches in sun and frost; 6/10. *C.* 'Ice Dance' is similar in habit but more dramatically variegated, and a better garden plant, tolerant of both sun and frost; 9/10.

C. muskingumensis
Palm leaf sedge
Most sedges have basal leaves and this is quite different in having erect stems, the leaves radiating from their sides, making the whole thing bear a superficial resemblance to a palm. A native of damp woodlands and meadows, spreading slowly by rhizomes. Capable of making large drifts. Effective groundcover. It is deciduous and the whole plant takes on shades of yellow ochre in autumn. 'Little Midge' is dwarf at 23cm (9in) with very narrow leaves; 8/10. 'Oehme' has leaves that gradually assume golden-yellow margins; 7/10. 'Silberstreif' is similar but has white-variegated leaves; 7/10. 'Wachtposten' is slightly taller than the typical plant, with yellowish green leaves; 5/10.

C. ornithopoda
Bird's foot sedge
Usually grown in its variegated form, 'Variegata', which is similar to *C. oshimensis* 'Variegata' but smaller and completely deciduous. Best in dampish soil in semi-shade; 7/10.

↕ 25cm/10in

↔ 30cm/12in

✺ late spring–midsummer

Z 6

C. oshimensis 'Evergold' AGM (C. o. 'Aureovariegata', 'Old Gold', 'Variegata')

This popular and easily grown sedge forms dense tufts of sprawling, undulating, shiny narrow leaves that are deep dark green with a broad central stripe of creamy yellow. The flowers are of little ornamental value. Best in some shade and never happy in hot climates. Sometimes erroneously attributed to C. hachijoensis; 10/10. **'Variegata'** is similar but white-variegated; 9/10.

Carex oshimensis 'Evergold'

↕ 23cm/9in

↔ indefinite

✺ late spring–early summer

Z 7

C. panicea

Carnation grass

Similar to C. flacca in its blue leaves but smaller and lacking the running habit; it is the better garden plant. Flowerheads chocolate brown. Ordinary soil in sun or shade; 6/10.

↕ 90cm/36in

↔ 90cm/36in

✺ mid-spring–early summer

Z 5

C. pendula

Pendulous sedge, weeping sedge

A coarse evergreen sedge with bold, pleated leaves forming dense tussocks and producing tall, arching stems from which hang jade-green catkins. Sows itself freely and can be difficult to eradicate. Usually relegated to the wilder parts of the garden, its architectural qualities make it highly suitable for associating with buildings and paving. Most soils, sun or shade, wet or dry. Suitable for cutting; 7/10. **'Moonraker'** has young spring leaves of palest cream becoming rich creamy yellow with a few thin green stripes, gradually turning mid-green by the end of the summer but new, cream-coloured leaves are continually produced. Keeps its colouring best in cool climates; in hot climates it may not colour at all. Smaller than the typical form, but no less liberal in its seeding; the seedlings are similarly coloured; 8/10.

↕ 30cm/12in

↔ 30cm/12in

✺ late spring–midsummer

Z 7

C. petriei

Petrie's brown sedge

Often described as a smaller C. buchananii, it differs also in its loosely tufted, spreading (not upright) habit, and its more definitely red colouring. Happiest in dampish soil in sun when it will seed itself lightly; 7/10.

Carex petriei

↕	60cm/24in
↔	23cm/9in
✽	early–late summer
Z	6

C. phyllocephala

A fascinating Chinese sedge producing its leaves in whorls near the tops of cane-like stems, the little brown flowers appearing to sit on top of the highest whorl. Makes an unusual feature in woodland or shade; 8/10. **'Sparkler'** is stunningly variegated white and green. More tender than the species, it makes an excellent container or conservatory plant; 10/10.

↕	20cm/8in
↔	30cm/12in
✽	late spring–early summer
Z	6

C. plantaginea

Plantain-leaved sedge, broad-leaved sedge

A North American woodlander grown for its wide, pleated leaves topped in spring with a myriad of small creamy flowers. Cool shade, even under trees; reasonably tolerant of dry shade. Sometimes confused with the green form of *C. siderosticha* but differs in its clumping not running habit and in being wintergreen. Lovely with woodlanders with bold foliage, such as hostas and ferns, or with spring flowers; 8/10.

↕	1.5m/5ft
↔	30cm/12in
✽	late spring–early summer
Z	6

C. riparia

Greater pond sedge

The blue-grey-leaved wild form grows at the edges of ponds and rivers throughout the northern hemisphere. An aggressive colonizer, it is suitable for lakes not ponds; 0/10. **'Variegata'** grows to half the height, the new leaves emerging pure white in earliest spring, slowly turning green. Flowers are black and appear while the leaves are white, making a dramatic contrast. Wet ground or waterside, or in a submerged container. Any green leaves should be cut out at the roots; 9/10.

↕	30cm/12in
↔	30cm/12in
✽	early–midsummer
Z	7

C. siderosticha

Broad-leaved sedge

Very similar to *C. plantaginea* but deciduous and with a slowly spreading habit. This and its forms need moist, fertile soil and some shade. Excellent groundcovers in shade; sometimes prone to slug damage; 6/10. The name **'Variegata'** embraces two forms. The better known makes low, slowly spreading mats, 15cm (6in) high and 23cm (9in) across, of densely overlapping, thinly textured leaves, mid-green flushed pink at first, maturing pale green, margined and striped white. The other is slightly larger, the leaves striped white but greyish not green. The difference is only seen when both are grown together. Both 9/10. **'Kisokaido'** produces new leaves that are tipped with white in spring and early summer, later thinly striped with white; 9/10. **'Shima Nishiki'** is similar to 'Variegata', but with rich gold variegation; 10/10.

↕	90cm/36in
↔	60cm/24in
✽	late spring–late summer
Z	5

C. sylvatica

Wood sedge

Useful rather than beautiful, this is similar to *C. pendula* but smaller in all its parts. Clump-forming. Excellent under trees; 4/10.

↕	60cm/24in
↔	30cm/12in
✽	late spring–midsummer
Z	7

C. tenuiculmis (*C. secta* var. *tenuiculmis*)

Rich chocolate-brown leaves that arch elegantly. Best in damp or wet ground; 8/10.

C. testacea

Orange sedge, orange New Zealand sedge, trip-me-up

Forms rounded mounds of shiny narrow evergreen leaves of ocherous olive bronzy-yellow, turning almost orange in sun, almost green in shade. Sun or shade, but best in good, slightly moist soil. Readily distinguished from *C. dipsacea* by its light brown flowers and in that the flower stem continues to extend far beyond the foliage after flowering, possibly reaching 2m (6ft) in length; 7/10.

↕ 45cm/18in
↔ 30cm/12in
✱ late spring–midsummer
Z 7

C. trifida

Similar to *C. pendula* but not so tall and quite distinct in its upright spikes of large, fluffy, foxy-red flowers. It makes bold clumps of broad pleated leaves dark green above, silvery beneath; 6/10. **var. *chatamica***, New Zealand blue sedge, is a geographical variant dramatic in its intensely blue leaves. It has the same foxy-red flowers and reaches about half the size of the green-leaved form. Relatively newly introduced to the northern hemisphere, its exact hardiness has not yet been determined; 9/10.

↕ 1m/39in
↔ 60cm/24in
✱ late spring–midsummer
Z 7

Chasmanthium

North America and Mexico

A genus of six or eight perennial grasses notable for their panicles of rather flat, compressed spikelets.

C. latifolium (*Uniola latifolia*)

Wild oats, wood oats, northern sea oats

Valuable in woodland and shade, this loosely clump-forming North American native will succeed in sun, provided that there is enough moisture at its roots. Quite upright in sun, more lax in shade, though attractively so. It produces pendent oat-like spikelets which resemble lockets, jade green at first, gradually turning light brown and flattened and shiny as though they have been ironed, but hard as if carved from wood. Forms delicate tracery among more substantial woodlanders, such as hostas. Best in groups or drifts; 8/10.

↕ 90cm/36in
↔ 30cm/12in
✱ midsummer–early autumn
Z 4
✳ warm

Chimonobambusa

Mainly China

Bamboos that are best in damp soils in light shade. They are runners, but run least in cool climates. They tend to produce new canes late in the season and these can be cut back by frosts, so that plants may never attain any size. When happy they make dense clumps or drifts.

C. marmorea

Densely leafy, small bamboo which when happy bows down under the weight of its leaves. Leaves deep green, shiny on the upper surface. The canes have prominent nodes. Useful for screening and hedging, provided that a root barrier is used to control its spread; 8/10.

↕ 2m/6ft x 2cm/¾in
↔ 1.5m/5ft in 10 years
Z 6

Chionochloa Snow grass, New Zealand tussock

New Zealand and Australia

Genus of 20 tussock-forming grasses, closely related to pampas grass, mostly from alpine and sub-alpine regions. Several species other than those mentioned are cultivated in New Zealand.

C. conspicua

Hunangamoho grass

↕	2.2m/7ft
↔	90cm/36in
❀	late spring–early autumn
Z	8
⚘	warm

One of the most gorgeous of all grasses, but not hardy in all gardens. Forms dense clumps of narrow, upright, arching evergreen leaves with a well-defined midrib, from the midst of which arise slender stems bearing large open panicles of creamy white flowers. All books recommend growing it in the sunniest position possible but the best plants I have ever seen were in woodland. Better on damper soils. The foliage contrasts well with woodlanders such as hostas, while the flowers are seen at their best in sun against a dark background. Also looks good with hydrangeas. Dislikes root disturbance. Though rated a warm-season grower, I have had greatest success dividing it in late summer. Good for cutting; 11/10.

C. flavescens

Broad-leaf snow grass

↕	1.5m/5ft
↔	90cm/36in
❀	late spring–midsummer
Z	8
⚘	warm

Smaller-growing version of C. conspicua differing in its broader leaves, which are somewhat glaucous on their upper surface, in the lower-growing leaf mound, in the oblique (rather than upright) stance of the flowering stems and in the much more open flower plume. Spikelets cream-coloured. Needs a moist but well-drained, fertile soil. Very showy where it succeeds and suitable for cutting; 9/10. This and the next are sometimes confused due to the similarity of their names.

C. flavicans

↕	1.5m/5ft
↔	90cm/36in
❀	late spring–midsummer
Z	8
⚘	warm

Similar to C. flavescens but differs in its one-sided plumes and in the flowers being greenish at first, becoming cream-coloured before drying off to a rich tawny brown. Less fussy about soil than C. flavescens. Good for cutting; 9/10.

C. rubra

Red snow grass, red tussock

↕	1.5m/5ft
↔	75cm/30in
❀	late spring–midsummer
Z	7
⚘	warm

The only true grass with brown leaves and the dominant plant of the alpine desert in New Zealand's North Island, where it grows by the thousand making upright-divergent clumps with silvery clemisias and raoulias in the seep channels at their feet. The stiff evergreen leaves are narrow and of a bright, foxy red, while the diffuse, airy panicles, borne just above the foliage, bear small chaffy parchment-coloured spikelets, like little swarms of insects. Grows best in damp soils but needs sun to colour well: the colouring is most intense in winter; 8/10.

Chondropetalum

Mostly South Africa
Genus of 10 species of restios.

C. tectorum

↕ 1.2m/4ft

↔ 30cm/12in

✿ early summer–early autumn

Z 8

A rush-like restio from marshy places forming dense tussocks of upright, dark green stems without any perceptible leaves. The newly emerging stems are clad in dark brown sheaths, so that as the stem extends the sheaths produce alternate bands of dark brown and rich green. Male and female flowers on different plants, but both look much the same and are borne at the tips of the stems in small, light brown clusters. Grows best in damp soils and will tolerate shade but still needs good light. It dislikes high fertility in the soil. It is difficult but not impossible to propagate by division as the roots resent disturbance, but can readily be raised from smoke-treated seed. Excellent in containers; 8/10.

Chusquea Foxtail bamboo

South America

Genus of 120 or so highly desirable bamboos from the high Andes, where they grow in forest clearings often shrouded in mist. In cultivation they dislike hot, dry conditions, growing best where the air is damp, as in moist woodland. They are also excellent in coastal areas and surprisingly wind-resistant. Best raised from seed when available as they resent root disturbance and it is often fatal to try to divide or move established clumps.

Chusquea culeou

↕ 6m/20ft x 2.5cm/1in

↔ 1.8m/6ft in 10 years

Z 7

C. culeou AGM

There are several clones, arising from different seed collections and not distinguished by name. Typically, a tall, very leafy bamboo with thick solid canes bearing most of its leaves in the upper half and usually bowing under the weight of the foliage. Newly emerging canes are wrapped in cream- or parchment-coloured sheaths making a great feature. Distinct from other bamboos in its branching, the branches being very fine and disposed around two-thirds of the cane; 10/10.

Coix

Tropical Asia
Genus of 6 annual or perennial grasses.

C. lacryma-jobi
Job's tears

↕ 60cm/24in

↔ 30cm/12in

✿ midsummer–early autumn

Z 9

❋ warm

Frost-tender grass from tropical Asia, cultivated for its huge, showy seeds once used for necklaces and rosaries. Needs a long, hot growing season to fruit well. In cool climates, sow it under glass and pot on regularly so that it does not receive any check to its growth. Plant it out in a really hot position, preferably at the foot of a sunny wall. When happy it makes a sprawly, large-leaved plant, bearing its pale grains in quite small panicles. Perennial and can be overwintered under glass; 8/10.

Cortaderia Pampas grass

Argentina, New Zealand and New Guinea

About 24 mostly large, coarse, tussock-forming evergreen grasses with large, showy panicles. All are best planted where they can be seen against a dark background such as pines or laurels with the sun beside or behind them. Best in sun in well-drained, moisture-retentive soils. The larger forms of *C. selloana* are too big for all but the largest gardens. *C. selloana* is only rated as zone 5 in the USA. However, for those who live in cold winter areas two new species, *C. patagonica* and *C. uspellata*, may give hope as they come from provenances where they have to endure extremely cold winters. They are reported to have blue foliage and to be free-flowering.

Cortaderia fulvida

↕	2.4m/8ft
↔	1.2m/4ft
✳	early–late summer
Z	8
❄	warm

C. fulvida

Kakaho

This New Zealand species makes huge mounds of rather untidy leaves and has tall stems bearing great fluffy plumes of delicious flamingo pink or clean white. Needs a warm, sunny place; 8/10.

C. richardii AGM

New Zealand pampas grass, toe-toe (pronounced 'toy-toy')

Quite different from the autumn-flowering Argentinian species and valued for its early flowering. Forms large tussocks of handsome broad, smooth, upward-arching leaves and produces neat, one-sided creamy plumes that gradually fade to white, on tall, arching stems. Any soil in sun; 10/10.

↕	2.4m/8ft
↔	90cm/36in
✳	early–midsummer
Z	8
❄	warm

Cortaderia richardii

C. selloana

Argentinian pampas grass

Varieties of *C. selloana* have the largest and showiest panicles of any hardy grasses but also make the largest mounds of foliage and so are not suitable for all gardens. They all form large rounded tussocks of arching, evergreen foliage; the leaves are edged with retrorse teeth, so you can plunge your hand into the heart of the clump without harm, but will be cut to the bone trying to draw it out – always wear tough leather gloves when handling pampas grasses. The plumes are silken to begin with, but gradually fill out and become fluffy. They are produced in mid- and late summer in the USA, but usually not until autumn in the UK. None will flower freely until well established. Although mostly hardy in Britain they are only rated as hardy to zone 5 in the USA. Plants of *C. selloana* are either male or female, most selections being females, which have the showiest flowers. Where both sexes are grown, seedlings may occur.

↕	3m/10ft
↔	1m/39in
✳	early–mid-autumn
Z	7
❄	warm

Pampas grasses look well when grown with *Kniphofia*, especially the stronger growing sorts such as the brilliant orange *K. rooperi*, *K. uvaria* var. *nobilis* or *K.* 'Samuel's Sensation', or set against the silvery-blue foliage of cardoons and with cannas in variety.

'**Albolineata**' ('Silver Stripe') is a small growing variety with leaves edged and striped white. More tender than other white, variegated forms; 10/10. '**Aureolineata**' ('Gold Band', 'Gold Banded') AGM is a strong grower with leaves margined and striped old gold; 10/10. '**Gold Band**', see 'Aureolineata'. '**Monstrosa**' is probably the tallest of the varieties grown for flower, the plumes reaching 3m (10ft). They are the whitest in flower; 10/10. '**Pink Feather**' is a seed strain with supposedly pink flowers; 5/10. '**Pumila**' AGM, dwarf pampas grass, is a free-flowering variety, the plumes not usually exceeding 1.5m (5ft) in height; 10/10. '**Rendatleri**' is famous for its pink plumes held well above the foliage. The stems break easily in strong winds; 9/10. '**Silver Beacon**' has leaves margined and striped white. The flower stems are purple; 9/10. '**Silver Comet**' has leaves margined and striped white; 9/10. The leaves of '**Silver Fountain**' are margined and striped white with green flower stems. Far larger than 'Albolineata'; 10/10. '**Silver Stripe**', see 'Albolineata'. '**Sunningdale Silver**' AGM is an old variety that has stood the test of time, with fuller plumes than 'Monstrosa' and a taller leaf mound, but ultimately about the same height; 10/10. '**White Feather**' is a seed strain producing plants with white flowers; 6/10.

Cortaderia selloana 'Sunningdale Silver'

Cymophyllus fraseri see Carex fraseri (page 33)

Cyperus Umbrella sedges, umbrella plants

Mainly tropics and subtropics

A distinct group of sedges named because of the leaf-like bracts that radiate outwards from the tops of the stems, like the ribs of an umbrella. Some also have basal leaves but many have only vestigial leaves reduced to small bracts clinging to the stems. All are natives of wet places and need to be grown with their feet in water or in wet ground. Easily increased by seed, division in spring or upper stem cuttings rooted in wet sand or water.

C. alternifolius

Umbrella plant

The most popular umbrella sedge, often used as a house or conservatory plant. There are no basal leaves, and the triangular stems carry quite wide, flat, leaf-like bracts just beneath the insignificant flowers. 'Variegata' is a form with the bracts somewhat white-striped. The green-leaved form can be grown in gardens in the warmer parts of Britain. *C. involucratus* is similar or may be the same; 7/10.

↕	1m/39in
↔	30cm/12in
✹	all year
Z	9

Cyperus alternifolius

C. eragrostis

Pale galingale

The least exciting sort but useful for its greater hardiness. The whole plant is pale green and produces basal leaves which are almost as tall as the flowering stems, thereby rather robbing the leaf-like bracts of their conspicuousness. Produces relatively few leafy bracts. Damp soil; 5/10.

↕	60cm/24in
↔	23cm/9in
✹	midsummer–early autumn
Z	7

C. longus

Galingale

A dense, vigorous, frost-hardy plant that increases rapidly, forming colonies in wet soil or at the water's edge. The stems and whorls of extraordinarily long leaf-like bracts are shiny deep green and the branched flowerheads are reddish brown and quite conspicuous. Can be invasive. Makes a fine foil for waterlily pads and the bold leaves of darmeras, rodgersias and waterside ligularias; 7/10.

↕	1.2m/4ft
↔	60cm/24in
✹	late summer–late autumn
Z	7

Cyperus longus

C. papyrus AGM

Papyrus, Egyptian paper reed

Often smaller in cultivation, this is still the giant of the genus and one of the most handsome of all cultivated plants, essential for evoking the atmosphere of the tumescent tropics. It has no basal leaves and lacks the whorl of leaf-like bracts that make most other species showy. Instead, it produces huge tufts of thread-like flower stalks each ending in a cluster of brown spikelets atop stiff, triangular stems; 10/10.

↕	4.5m/15ft
↔	1m/39in
✹	late spring–late autumn
Z	9

Dactylis Cocksfoot grass, orchard grass

Europe, North Africa, temperate Asia
A single species of coarse, tufted perennial grass.

D. glomerata 'Variegata'

Striped cocksfoot grass, orchard grass
This has conspicuously white-striped leaves that tend to look their best in spring and autumn, often going into semi-dormancy in summer. When it does this it is best cut down to encourage a new flush of leaves. The flowers are unattractive little clumps of spikelets and it does not flower freely. Easily grown in most soils, in sun or shade; 6/10.

↕	30cm/12in
↔	15cm/6in
✻	late spring–midsummer
Z	5
❋	cool

Deschampsia

Cool temperate regions
A genus of about 40 species of perennial grasses.

↕	1m/39in
↔	60cm/24in
✻	late spring–mid-autumn
Z	4
❋	cool

D. cespitosa *(Aira cespitosa)*

Tufted hair grass
This species is in the first rank of ornamental grasses, both for its beauty and for its utility. It forms dense tussocks of dark green leaves with upright-divergent and sometimes pendulous flowering stems bearing loose panicles of tiny spikelets that start silvery green and turn yellow or bronze and finally hay-coloured. These are borne from late spring until the end of summer and usually continue to contribute to the garden even in winter. It grows happily in most soils, even clays, in sun or in shade. Rabbits love it. There are numerous named varieties, the majority being European selections that do not always do well in North America, especially in warmer regions where homegrown American selections perform better. Looks well in semi-shade with pure blue *Corydalis flexuosa* 'China Blue' (or 'Purple Leaf') at its feet; with *Nectaroscordum siculum* or the shorter *N. bulgaricum*; or with *Veronicastrum virginicum* or the taller spires of foxgloves, like *Digitalis ferruginea*. The species and its forms are all rated 10/10, except 'Northern Lights' 2/10 and 'Fairy's Joke' 1/10.

'Bronzeschleier' (bronze veil) is the best-known selection, with bronzy spikelets on 90cm (3ft) stems and pendulous panicle branches. One of the better cultivars for warmer climates. More prone to foliar rust than other selections. **'Fairy's Joke'** is a viviparous form, producing plantlets where there should be flowers. An ugly curiosity. **'Goldgehänge'** (golden pendant, golden shower) is a lovely variety with golden spikelets. It is not so tall as 'Goldschleier' and flowers later, starting in midsummer. The branches of the panicle are pendulous, giving the flowerhead a weeping effect. **'Goldschleier'** (golden veil) has attractive silvery green panicles in early summer that quickly turn golden; slightly taller than most. Lovely massed, and effective well into winter. **'Goldstaub'** (gold dust) is a short variety with golden panicles on green stems. **'Goldtau'** (golden dew) is also short with panicles that start silvery green and slowly turn golden yellow. It is good paired with 'Goldschleier', which flowers earlier and is taller, and lovely with *Achillea* 'Lachsschönheit'. **'Northern Lights'** is less than half the size of

Deschampsia cespitosa 'Goldgehänge' (above), 'Goldschleier' (below).

*Deschampsia cespitosa
'Goldtau'*

↕	75cm/30in
↔	23cm/9in
❁	early–midsummer
Z	4
☀/❄	cool

other selections and dramatically variegated creamy white. It seems to flourish in nurserymen's polytunnels but I've never succeeded with it in the garden. Reverts badly. **'Schottland'** (Scotland) A vigorous, robust variety with extra-dark green leaves and flowering stems that reach 90cm (3ft). **'Tardiflora'** flowers later than other varieties, and is is useful for that reason alone. **'Tautraeger'** (dew bearer) is short-growing with panicles that are almost blue when they open, ripening to a rich straw colour. **'Waldeschatt'** (forest shade) has dark brown panicles, unlike any other variety.

A problem with the named selections is that they tend to seed themselves back into the parent clump and, being identical in leaf, pass unnoticed until they flower, at which point the clump needs to be dug up and divided and the errant seedlings discarded, or a new plant bought that is true to name.

D. flexuosa
Wavy hair grass
A grass of exceptional beauty, forming low tufts of dark, more or less evergreen leaves of thread-like fineness overtopped by airy panicles of shimmering silvery brown spikelets. It is native to sandy or peaty acid soils and will not grow on alkaline or chalky soils. It is usually found in dry conditions in woodland clearings, but can sometimes be found in damp or even wet habitats. Though generally tuft-forming, it is inclined to run in sandy soils; 10/10. **'Tatra Gold'** has bilious yellow-green leaves and reddish brown flowers in early summer. Just the right shade of yellow to look dreadful with practically everything; 4/10.

Dichromena see Rhynchorspora (page 75)

Elegia
South Africa
Genus of 35 species of restios, 17 of which are natives to South Africa. A few of these are occasionally grown in gardens.

↕	2.1m/7ft
↔	1.5m/5ft
❁	midsummer–early autumn
Z	8

E. capensis
Glorious restio from the fynbos vegetation of South Africa, forming upright clumps of green stems covered from top to bottom with whorls of thread-like green branches and topped by small spikes of brown flowers. Bears a superficial resemblance to an overgrown mare's tail (*Equisetum*) but is readily distinguished by the presence of chocolate-brown papery bracts, which enclose the branches at first. Worth any amount of trouble to establish, it needs damp soil in sun and will not tolerate any fertilizer or manure; 10/10.

Elymus Lyme grass, wild rye, wheatgrass

Northern temperate areas and Asia

Genus of about 150 clumping or running perennial grasses.

E. hispidus

Blue wheatgrass

A loosely tufted more or less evergreen perennial grass, grown for the intense blueness of its narrow leaves, which are held erect at first but become more spreading as the season advances. The panicle is a dense, wheat-like spike of the same blue as the leaves but quickly fades through straw yellow to beige. Needs well-drained soil in sun, but even then is prone to foliar rusts. Grows better in the cooler north of England than the south and tends to go into summer dormancy in areas with hot summer nights. Goes well with purple foliage, and flowers in every shade from pink to darkest purple; 9/10.

Elymus hispidus

↕	60cm/24in
↔	30cm/12in
❁	early–midsummer
z	5
✳	cool

E. magellanicus

Less intensely blue than *E. hispidus*, and with a lax, spreading habit, this grass from the southern tip of South America cannot be considered soundly perennial in Britain, often behaving as an annual or biennial. Flowers and flower stems are the same colour as the leaves. Grows in most soils, in sun; 5/10.

↕	15cm/6in
↔	30cm/12in
❁	early–late summer
z	5
✳	cool

Eragrostis Love grass

Mainly from tropical and subtropical regions

Genus of over 300 annual and perennial grasses. Those featured here are good for cutting.

E. chloromelas

Boer love grass

Forms a flowing mound of greyish to nearly blue in the best forms, almost hair-like leaves and produces long slender, arching stems bearing delicate panicles, lovely both in detail and from a distance. In winter the leaves bleach out, but the airy panicles remain greyish. Self seeds and may be a nuisance; 7/10.

↕	1.2m/4ft
↔	30cm/12in
❁	midsummer–late autumn
z	7
✳	warm

E. curvula

African love grass, weeping love grass

Similar to *E. chloromelas* but smaller. Differs most notably in its overall colouring, which is dark green. The panicles are generally similar to those of *E. chloromelas* and are borne on similarly long stems, but grey-green rather than greyish. Easy in most soils in sun but can seed around and become a menace. Good in pots where the flowing foliage can weep over the edges; 7/10.

↕	90cm/36in
↔	30cm/12in
❁	summer–autumn
z	7
✳	warm

↕	60cm/24in
↔	30cm/12in
❋	late summer–early winter
Z	5
✳	warm

↕	1.2m/4ft
↔	30cm/12in
❋	late summer–early·winter
Z	5
✳	warm

E. spectabilis

Purple love grass, tumble grass

Similar to *E. trichodes* but with smaller panicles and bright, almost iridescent violet spikelets. Almost any soil in sun; 8/10.

E. trichodes

Sand love grass

This spectacular grass produces large, diffuse panicles bearing myriad tiny shimmering amethyst spikelets; the panicles are unusual in that they are narrowest at the bottom and widest at the top and the flowers are often borne so freely that they obscure the foliage. 'Bend' love grass is the most spectacular of the love grasses, having even larger panicles with reddish bronze spikelets. A single flowerhead can measure as much as 60cm (24in) long and 20cm (8in) across. It is not as wonderful in the garden as it might sound because the stems are lax and the flowerheads tend to fall away from the plant centre, leaning on surrounding vegetation for support or falling on the ground. Lovely for picking and will last for years once dried. Easy in most soils in sun; 9/10.

Erianthus see Saccharum (page 75)

Eriophorum Cotton grass

Northern temperate and arctic regions

About 20 species of moisture-loving perennials in the sedge family grown for their showy seedheads, which resemble balls of cotton wool. All come from acid swamps or sphagnum bogs. In cultivation they grow in moist acid soil or with their feet in water. Readily increased by seed or division.

↕	60cm/24in
↔	30cm/12in
❋	late spring–late summer
Z	4

E. angustifolium

Cotton grass, common cotton grass

Dark narrow leaves and slender stems of unremarkable flowers are followed by fluffy white cotton-wool seedheads. Spreads by far-running rhizomes. Best grown in drifts. Showiest with the sun beyond it; 9/10.

↕	70cm/28in
↔	30cm/12in
❋	late spring–midsummer
Z	4

E. latifolium

Broad-leaved cotton grass

Similar to *E. angustifolium* but slightly taller and clump-forming; 9/10.

Fargesia Chinese mountain bamboo

Chinese Himalayas

A large genus of elegant bamboos, most clump-forming and many very cold-hardy and wind-tolerant, though lose their leaves in the worst of gales. The two species included here are clump-formers of exceptional beauty. They are small enough to be grown in most gardens. They need moist soil – they roll their leaves when dry and it is vital to apply water immediately. They look their best sheltered from cold winds. Excellent in pots.

F. murielae AGM (Arundinaria murielae, Arundinaria spathacea, Fargesia spathacea, Sinarundinaria murielae, Thamnocalamus spathaceus)

Probably the most widely planted bamboo, this has light green canes that fade to yellow, and an abundance of pale green leaves that cause the canes to arch and bow down under their weight creating a fountain-like effect. It has been flowering recently giving rise to several new varieties with specific merits: 'Harewood' is dwarf at 90cm (36in) and ideal for large pots and tubs. 'Jumbo' is taller, to 3.5m (11ft), with wider leaves. 'Simba' AGM has closely packed canes and grows to 2m (6ft). 'Thyme' is similar but only reaches 1.5m (5ft). All 10/10.

↕ 2.5m/8ft x 1.3cm/½in

↔ 90cm/3ft in 10 years

Z 4

F. nitida

Similar to the *F. murielae* except that the leaves are generally smaller and the canes quickly turn purple. Possibly even more cold-tolerant. 'Eisenach' has canes that curve as they arise from the ground, and then straighten; 'Nymphenburg' AGM has longer, narrower leaves and a more pronounced weeping habit. All 10/10.

↕ 3m/10ft x 1.3cm/½in

↔ 90cm/3ft in 10 years

Z 4

Festuca Fescue

Temperate zones worldwide

Genus of about 300 tufted perennial grasses. Apart from those used in lawns, garden species are all tuft-forming and mostly have leaves in differing shades of blue or blue-green. They need to be grown where they are in sun virtually all day, in sharply drained soil, and are generally not a success in heavy soils. The blue or blue-green of the leaves is produced by a waxy coating which is there to protect the leaves against excessive sunlight: beneath the wax the leaves are deep green. In winter, when they no longer need this protection, the underlying green is more visible. Most dislike hot, humid summers, which can make them look miserable. The plants should be cut down in early spring to encourage vigorous new leaves, and should be divided every three or four years to maintain their vigour. There is much confusion about the naming of the popular blue types, which various authors assign to various species, but here they are treated as cultivars of *F. glauca*.

F. amethystina

Similar to *F. glauca* but larger and with fine bluish leaves with a slight hint of mauve; 9/10.

↕ 45cm/18in

↔ 30cm/12in

❋ late spring–midsummer

Z 7

❋ cool

↕	30cm/12in
↔	23cm/9in
❄	early–midsummer
Z	5
✳	cool

↕	25cm/10in
↔	15cm/6in
❄	late spring–midsummer
Z	5
✳	cool

↕	30cm/12in
↔	1.8m/6ft
❄	late spring–midsummer
Z	5
✳	cool

↕	15cm/6in
↔	15cm/6in
❄	summer
Z	5
✳	cool

F. gautieri
Bearskin fescue
Extraordinary little green fescue that makes dark green mats resembling bearskin and bears yellowish flowers on silvery stems. Though seemingly ideal for rock gardens, its fine running rhizomes can get in among rocks, paving or other plants and are almost impossible to eradicate; 9/10. **'Pic Carlit'** is a lower-growing selection; 8/10. *F. eskia* is similar; 9/10.

F. glauca (*F. ovina* var. *glauca, F. cinerea, F. cinerea* var. *glauca*)
Blue fescue
Generally short-lived natives of Europe. The leaves are usually glaucous blue or silvery blue; at first the upright flower stems and flowerheads are the same colour as the leaves but they soon bleach to a light straw colour. They may be removed by clipping over with shears. Lovely with spring bulbs and with flowers or foliage in shades of pink, blue, mauve or purple. Their short-lived nature makes them unsuitable for mass planting, except perhaps as bedding; 8–10/10.

The following are generally available. **'Aprilgrün'** leaves fresh green; 8/10. **'Azurit'** leaves blue-silver; 8/10. **'Blaufink'** (blue finch) leaves more silver than blue; 9/10. **'Blaufuchs'** (blue fox) AGM similar to 'Blaufink'; 9/10. **'Blauglut'** (blue glow) again similar to 'Blaufink'; 9/10. **'Blausilber'** (blue-silver) leaves more blue than silver; one of the best selections; 8/10. **'Caesia'** leaves silvery blue; 9/10. An early selection and still excellent. **var. *coxii*** leaves blue-silver, seldom flowers, a little smaller than most; 10/10. **'Elijah Blue'** leaves silvery blue. A larger, more vigorous and longer-lived selection than most. Probably the best of the blues; 10/10. **'Golden Toupee'** is a yellow-leaved seedling found in a batch of blue ones. Originally thrown on the bonfire, where it should have stayed. Leaves yellow with a blue cast; 5/10. **'Harz'** leaves a deep, dull blue, a heavier colour than most and useful as a contrast to the more silvery selections; 6/10. **'Mereblau'** leaves sea-green with further green over- (or under-) tones. A good foil to bluer selections. *minima* leaves silvery blue. Makes tufts about half the size of other blue-leaved selections; 7/10. **'Seeigel'** (sea urchin) spiky clumps of olive-green leaves, makes an interesting contrast with blue-leaved selections; 6/10. **'Solling'** leaves silvery grey; 7/10. *F. valesiaca* is similar. It is usually grown in the form **'Silbersee'** (silver sea, sometimes sold as Severn Seas), one of the most intensely silvery blue selections; 9/10.

F. rubra
Red fescue, creeping red fescue
A creeping evergreen grass spreading by means of wiry rhizomes. The green-leaved forms have been developed for use in lawns and need good, fertile soil to flourish. **'Jughandle'** and **'Molate'** are good blue-leaved selections, which are used in the same way as other blue-leaved grasses; 7/10.

F. vivipara
This species from northern Europe is similar to *F. glauca* in its blue-green leaves but produces tiny plantlets instead of flowers. A curiosity for rock gardens or sinks. **'In'** is a dwarf form to 5cm (2½in). Both 7/10.

Glyceria Manna grass, sweet manna grass

Northern temperate regions, Australia, New Zealand and South America
Genus of about 40 perennial grasses mostly from damp or wet places, and mostly with running rootstocks.

G. maxima

↕	2.4m (8ft)
↔	1m/39in
✳	mid–late summer
Z	5
✳	cool

Usually grown in the form **var. *variegata*** ('Variegata'), which has leaves striped brightly creamy-white and green, strongly tinted pink or purplish in spring. The open, airy flowerheads, which are of little ornamental value, are held high above the leaf mound, which usually grows no more than 90cm (36in) tall. If the leaves deteriorate in late summer, cut them down to encourage a new flush. Any soil, so long as it is moist, or shallow water; 10/10.

Hakonechloa Hakone grass

Honshu, Japan
A single species from the region around Mount Hakone in Honshu, Japan's main island, and named after that mountain.

H. macra

↕	30cm/12in
↔	30cm/12in
✳	late summer–early autumn
Z	5
✳	warm

One of the most elegant grasses, forming slowly increasing mounds of cascading mid-green foliage. When planted en masse it makes carpets of weed-suppressing greenery that wave in the wind like a field of corn. The tiny flowers are produced in a limp, open panicle that tends to rest on top of the leaf mound; at about the same time, the leaves start assuming their autumn colours, becoming first tinged with pink and then with vinous reddish purple. The whole plant turns sere-brown in winter, but the spring buds are again dark reddish purple. Best in moisture-retentive, well-drained soils with an abundance of organic matter, in sun or shade for part of the day; 9/10.

Hakonechloa macra 'Alboaurea'

Three variegated forms are grown. **'Alboaurea'** AGM has leaves variegated rich golden yellow and green with occasional white flecks and markings, and red streaks or flushes. **'Aureola'** AGM is variegated rich golden yellow and green, and creates the brighter effect of the two. **'Mediovariegata'** ('Albovariegata') grows a little larger and is striped green and cream, the cream fading to near white by the end of the summer, sooner in hotter climates. All 11/10.

The gold forms look well with the blood-red leaves of *Imperata cylindrica* 'Rubra', the browns of many New Zealand sedges and sedums such as *S. telephium* 'Lynda et Rodney' or *Cimicifuga simplex* 'Brunette', the vivid purple of purple sage, and with most plants with blue or silvery foliage, including other grasses.

Helictotrichon

Temperate northern hemisphere
About 100 perennial grasses found in open spaces. Only the following is important in gardens. It is also good for cutting.

H. sempervirens AGM

Blue oat grass
Rather larger than the blue fescues (*Festuca*), and not quite so intensely blue as *Elymus hispidus*, this evergreen, clump-forming grass makes a more shapely plant, the narrow, tapering grey-blue leaves radiating outwards from the centre like a fibre-optic toy. The oat-like flowers are borne in an open, one-sided panicle, grey-blue at first quickly becoming pale straw and bleaching to almost white. The stems and chaffy, empty seed cases remain attractive until late summer. It will not flower reliably in warm climates; 10/10. var. *pendulum* ('Pendulum') has arching flower stems and is not so showy; 8/10. 'Saphirsprudel' has leaves of a deeper, less silvery blue; 10/10. All need a sunny position in well-drained soil and suffer from the fact that ants like to make their nests in them, usually killing them and thus making them unsuitable for mass planting. Be cautious with proprietory ant remedies as many are phytotoxic.

- ↕ 1.2m/4ft
- ↔ 60cm/24in
- ❀ early–midsummer
- Z 4
- cool

Hibanobambusa (x *Phyllosasa*)

Unique among cultivated bamboos in being a hybrid, its putative parents being *Phyllostachys nigra* 'Henonis' and *Sasa veitchi*. It has the large canes and swollen nodes of the phyllostachys together with the large leaves of the sasa.

H. tranquillans

A vigorous bamboo with canes that curve as they emerge from the ground and then grow straight upwards. They bear large, dark green leaves the weight of which makes them tend to bend outwards. The handsome foliage seems impervious to wind and weather. Needs good fertile soil and grows best in a little shade and shelter; 8/10. 'Shiroshima' AGM, the form usually grown, has leaves clearly and conspicuously striped in shades of cream and green, often tinted pink or purple in strong sunlight. It has the largest and most brightly variegated leaves of any hardy bamboo; 10/10.

- ↕ 5m/16ft x 2cm/¾in
- ↔ 3m/10ft in 10 years
- Z 8

Holcus

Eurasia and Africa
Genus of 6 species of annual and perennial grasses.

H. mollis

Yorkshire fog, creeping soft grass
Only grown in its variegated form **'Variegatus'** ('Albovariegatus'), a diminutive grass growing no more than 15cm (6in) tall and forming loose, sprawling mats. It spreads slowly by runners just on or just below the surface and can easily be controlled. The leaves, which are always short and close together on the stems, are deep green at the centre and broadly margined in clean, bright white. The flowers are greenish white with a mauvish cast but are of no decorative value. Happiest in dampish places in acid soils. In warm climates it should be grown in some shade but even then may become dormant in summer; 8/10.

- ↕ 75cm/30in (in flower)
- ↔ spreading
- ❀ early–late summer
- Z 5
- cool

Hordeum

Temperate areas

About 40 annual and perennial grasses with barley-like flowerheads native to dry habitats around the temperate world. Only the following is commonly grown, usually as an annual.

↕	30cm/12in
↔	23cm/9in
✼	early–midsummer
Z	5

H. jubatum

Squirrel-tail barley

A highly ornamental grass with barley-like heads, the long silky awns often tinted shimmering crimson or pink. As the flowers turn into seeds, the head develops a spiral twist along the floral axis and soon shatters. If the heads are wanted for drying they should be picked before they are fully open. Though usually grown as an annual, it will make a loosely tufted, short-lived perennial. Mixes well with garden pinks and bearded irises and enjoys the same conditions; 10/10.

Hordeum jubatum

Hystrix

Temperate regions of both hemispheres

About 6 perennial grasses named from the Greek term for a porcupine.

↕	90cm/36in
↔	30cm/12in
✼	early–midsummer
Z	4
✼	cool

H. patula

Bottlebrush grass

An interesting grass to grow in small, intimate gardens but too untidy in leaf and too quiet in its flowering to make a show in a larger landscape. Forms loose tufts of unremarkable leaves and produces long-awned flowerheads that somewhat resemble bottlebrushes, green flushed rosy pink at first, fading to tan and then bleaching out for the winter. Grows best in moist fertile soils in woodland; 5/10.

Hystrix patula

Imperata

Mostly tropical

About 8 species of tropical grasses with a few species from cooler climates. All spread by underground stems.

↕	38cm/15in
↔	15cm/6in
✼	seldom flowers
Z	6
✼	warm

I. cylindrica

The wild form from Japan, China and Korea is a vigorously invasive grass with upright mid-green leaves stained brown, especially towards the tip. It is best avoided in gardens; 2/10. 'Rubra' ('Red Baron'), Japanese blood grass, is the most brilliantly coloured of all grasses. The leaves, which begin to emerge in early spring, are held erect and are at first a yellowish green with the tip just touched with red, but as the season advances the blood drains downwards, staining the whole leaf blood-red, the colour attaining its

Imperata cylindrica 'Rubra'

greatest intensity in midsummer to early autumn. Best in sun in moisture-retentive soil; increases rather too slowly. The most remarkable effects are achieved when it is planted so that the sun shines through it from behind and the leaves glow with borrowed effulgence, like a glass of red wine held to the light. Lovely with *Hakonechloa macra* 'Aureola' or *Alopecurus pratensis* 'Aureomarginata' or blue-leaved grasses such as *Helictotrichon sempervirens,* and with other silver- or grey-leaved plants and with pink or purple flowers; 10/10.

Indocalamus

About 25 bamboos with running rhizomes which used to be included in *sasa.* The species included here does not run over vigorously and is usually easily controlled.

 60cm/24in x 5mm/¼in

↔ 1.2m/4ft in 10 years

❀ sporadic

Z 8

I. tessellatus AGM
This has the largest leaves of any hardy cultivated bamboo. The canes bend under their weight, making it a low-growing plant, although the canes are about 90cm (36in) long. Suitable for groundcover; 10/10. **f. *hamadae*** has slightly longer leaves, sometimes 60cm (24in) long, on more upright canes, making it much taller at 1.5m (5ft) high. Plants tend to make rounded bushes and may be used as specimens; 9/10.

Ischyrolepis Cape reed
South Africa and southern hemisphere
Genus of 48 species of restios, 15 of them from South Africa. The awkward-looking name is pronounced 'eyes-crow-lepis'. They look like a cross between a grass and a mare's tail (*Equisetum*) and are showy in their plant form rather than in their flowers. *I. subverticillata* has been in cultivation for over 100 years, mainly as a conservatory plant, though it can be cultivated out of doors in mild winter areas.

↕ 1.5m (5ft)

↔ 90cm/36in

❀ early–late summer

Z 8

I. subverticillata
Probably the most fascinating of the restios for the garden, this statuesque species throws up long, dark green stems bearing whorls of feathery, thread-like stems that cause the main stems to arch elegantly outwards under their weight. Small greenish yellow flowers are produced in summer, turning to greyish brown nutlets. Best grown in sun in moisture-retentive acid soils. Alternatively, can be grown in large containers and overwintered under cover if necessary; 10/10.

Juncus effusus

↕	30cm/12in
↔	30cm/12in
✿	mid–late summer
Z	3

↕	30cm/12in
↔	30cm/12in
✿	mid–late summer
Z	5

↕	75cm/30in
↔	30cm/12in
✿	mid–late summer
Z	4

↕	15cm/6in
↔	23cm/8in
✿	mid–late summer
Z	5

↕	1.2m/4ft
↔	75cm/18in
✿	mid–late summer
Z	4

↕	45cm/30in
↔	30cm/12in
✿	mid–late summer
Z	7

Juncus Rush

Throughout cool temperate regions

About 200 perennial grass-like plants from damp or wet habitats. They lack true leaves, their function being carried out by the cylindrical stems. The flowers are borne in small tufts about a third of the way up the stem and are of little ornamental value. Although indispensable in larger landscapes, few are worthy of gardens. Some produce forms with spirally twisted leaves, often known as corkscrew rushes. The clumps slowly fill up with dead stems so they need to be cut to the ground from time to time. Those featured here are suitable for cutting.

J. balticus 'Spiralis'
Corkscrew Baltic rush
This has spirally twisted stems looking like a bunch of overgrown green corkscrews sticking out of the mud, which some people find attractive. It runs at the roots forming drifts rather than clumps. In the USA this plant was for long sold as *J. effusus* 'Spiralis', which is clump-forming; 5/10.

J. decipiens 'Curly-wurly' (*J. decipiens* 'Spiralis')
This corkscrew rush has shiny, bright green spirally and often tightly twisted stems. Easily grown in wet soil; 3/10.

J. effusus
Common rush, soft rush
A vigorous clump-forming rush with dark green vertical stems making dense patches at the water's edge. 'Cuckoo' may be the same as 'Gold Strike'. 'Gold Strike' is an eyecatching American selection with longitudinally gold-striped stems. Grows taller in damp ground; 4/10. f. *spiralis* is another corkscrew rush with deep shining green stems and a clump-forming habit; 5/10. 'Unicorn' is a tetraploid corkscrew rush, larger in all its parts than the others and almost worth space in a pond in the garden; 6/10.

J. glomeratus 'Spiralis'
This is another corkscrew rush but in miniature, looking more like a ball of rusting wirewool than a clutch of corkscrews. Any damp soil. Also good in peat beds where it seeds itself around; 3/10.

J. inflexus
Hard rush, inflexible rush
Usually only seen in gardens in its corkscrew form, 'Afro', this is distinct in that its stems are grey, not green, and in that it will grow well in ordinary earth; 6/10.

J. patens 'Carman's Gray'
makes dense bundles of upright stems and is remarkable for the greyness of its stems and the copious profusion of its flowering. 'Elk Blue' is similar but bluer. Both 6/10.

Koeleria vallesiana

↕	23cm/9in
↔	23cm/9in
✿	early–midsummer
Z	6
✳	cool

Koeleria

America and Eurasia

Genus of annual or perennial grasses. The two species featured resemble each other and, to confuse things, look rather like some of the little blue fescues. The leaves differ, those of the fescues being usually rolled so that they appear round and very narrow, while those of the koelerias are broader and flatter, but the only infallible guide is the panicle. In the fescues this is a weedy little one-sided affair, while in the koelerias it is a dense spike. Both species are inclined to summer dormancy and should be planted where this can be overlooked. Best in light sandy or chalky soils in sun; not a success on very acid soils.

K. glauca
Blue hair grass

Makes dense clumps of soft blue-green leaves and produces showy spikes of flowers, at first the same colour as the leaves but soon fading to beige. Grows best on light sandy soils in sun. Suitable for cutting; 7/10. *K. vallesiana,* native to the limestone hills of southern Britain, is similar.

Lagurus

Mediterranean region

A genus of a single species.

↕	30cm/12in
↔	30cm/12in
✿	summer

L. ovatus AGM
Hare's tail

A delightful, free-flowering annual producing masses of flame-shaped flowerheads seemingly made of soft beige hairs with well-groomed long awns protruding from the shorter hairs, all pointing in the same direction. It makes a loosely tufted plant with short, hairy leaves. 'Bunny Tails', a dwarf form, grows to 15cm (6in) and is suitable for the front of a border. 'Nanus' is the same. All need a sunny place in well-drained soil. Flowering time can be varied by sowing seed at different times. All 9/10.

↕	30cm/12in
↔	23cm/9in
✿	late spring–midsummer

Lamarckia

Mediterranean region

A genus of a single species of annual grass, grown for its golden panicles.

Lamarckia aurea

L. aurea
Goldentop

An annual grass forming loosely tufted clumps. The spike-like flowerhead is quite distinct from other grasses in that the awns and spikelets, instead of pointing towards the tip, point backwards. The whole head is silky and yellow, sometimes becoming flushed with purple. In southern England it will flower in early summer from seed sown out of doors in spring, but earlier flowering can be achieved by starting plants under glass. Needs a sunny place in well-drained soil; 8/10.

Leymus racemosus

↕ 1.1m/42in

↔ 60cm/24in

❋ mid–late summer

Z 4

✳ cool

Leymus Lyme grass, blue lyme grass, wild rye

Northern temperate regions and one species in Argentina.
A genus of about 40 perennial grasses now including many formerly attributed to *Elymus*.

L. arenarius

Blue lyme grass

Grown for its electric blue leaves, this forms loosely tufted clumps or colonies and has a vigorously running root system: in the wild it binds sand dunes. The flower spikes, like elongated ears of wheat, are as blue as the leaves at first but quickly fade to pale scrubbed stone. In cold climates the whole plant turns yellow as winter approaches but in warmer areas it is virtually evergreen. Grows in most soils in sun. Like the majority of blue grasses, it looks remarkably effective in terracotta pots or against terracotta bricks or paving, and it is lovely as an underplanting to pale pink roses. Loses points for its aggressive root system; 8/10. *L. racemosus* is virtually indistinguishable.

Luzula Woodrush

Mainly from the cold temperate regions of the northern hemisphere.
About 80 mostly perennial grass-like plants closely allied to the true rushes and useful as groundcover in both wet and dry woodland gardens and in shade on most types of soil.

↕ 60cm/24in

↔ 30cm/12in

❋ late spring–early summer

Z 4

L. nivea

Snowy woodrush

Forms loosely tufted clumps of narrow quite upright leaves, lightly covered in silky white hairs, and spreads slowly by rhizomes. Off-white flowers are produced in open heads and rather detract from the effectiveness of the foliage. 'Snowbird' has whiter flowers. *L. luzulodies* 'Schneehäschen' (little snow hare) is similar also with whiter flowers. The all score 5/10.

Luzula sylvatica 'Taggart's Cream'

↕ 60cm/24in

↔ 30cm/12in

❋ late spring–midsummer

Z 5

L. sylvatica (*L. maxima*)

Greater woodrush

Forms slowly spreading clumps of broad evergreen foliage that gradually makes a weedproof carpet under trees, even in dry shade. The flowers are whitish at first, soon fading to brown; they are borne in flattened heads on upright stems in early summer. Named varieties are usually grown rather than the typical wild plant. 'Aurea' has leaves that turn an intense golden-yellow in the winter, but only in sun. 'Bromel' (so named for its supposed resemblance to the tuft at the top of a pineapple) is a tetraploid giant, larger in all its parts and producing its flowers atop 90cm (36in) stems; it is showy and vigorous. 'Hohe Tatra' has leaves that stand upright, creating a different effect on the woodland floor ('Aurea' is sometimes sold under this name). 'Marginata' is the commonest variety and has clean white edges to the leaves. 'Taggart's Cream' starts early into growth and has leaves that are pure white at first, gradually becoming cream, then green. Excellent in the winter garden where it can be hidden by other plants once its moment of glory is over. 'Wäldler' has brighter green, rather broader leaves than the others.

Melica Melic

Temperate regions, not Australia

About 70 perennial grasses. All are cool-season growers tending to summer dormancy and best planted where they are out of sight in summer. The foliage should be removed while dormant.

↕	1.2m/4ft
↔	30cm/12in
❀	late spring–early summer
Z	5
✻	cool

M. altissima

Siberian melic

The Siberian melic forms loose, often sprawling tufts of soft leaves. Erect flower panicles consist of loose spikes of one-sided showy florets followed by rice-like grains. 'Alba' has white florets. 'Atropurpurea' has mauve-purple florets followed by jet-black grains. All grow in most soils and tolerate light shade, often leaning on their neighbours for support. Suitable for cutting. They look good among silver leaves and harmonize well with the nacreous flowers of *Salvia turkestanica*. All 8/10.

M. transsilvanica is similar but smaller, with grey-green leaves and fluffy, purplish pink flowers. 'Atropurpurea' has delicious, deeper-coloured flowers; 8/10.

↕	60cm/24in
↔	30cm/12in
❀	late spring–early summer
Z	6
✻	cool

M. ciliata

Silky-spike melic

Forms tufts of light green leaves and produces neat cylindrical panicles of chaffy flowers, off-white later turning light biscuit in colour. Most soils in sun. Useful for its early flowers; 7/10.

↕	90cm/36in
↔	75cm/30in
❀	late spring–early summer
Z	6
✻	cool

M. macra

Grown for its chaffy, nearly white spikelets, abundantly produced relatively early in the year. It makes an excellent companion for *Stipa gigantea* and deschampsias, which flower in the same season. Easy in any fertile soil; 8/10.

↕	30cm/12in
↔	15cm/6in
❀	late spring–early summer
Z	5
✻	cool

M. nutans

Nodding melic

Grown for its thin, pale green leaves and its arching heads of small white flowers, but above all for the delicacy of the plant as a whole. Not in the first rank but useful as groundcover in light shade; 6/10.

↕	30cm/12in
↔	15cm/6in
❀	late spring–early summer
Z	5
✻	cool

M. uniflora

Wood melic

A delicate-looking woodland grass that forms loose, slowly spreading clumps of pale green arching leaves and stems. Tiny, dark spikelets are borne on thread-like stems in an open panicle, but are no more showy than the leaves; 5/10. f. *albida* has clean white flowers and is much more effective; 7/10. 'Variegata' is treasured for the subtlety of its greyish white variegation and the fact that it flourishes in shaded and woodland gardens, its quiet colouring being appropriate to the quieter mood of such places. Slow to increase and best planted in drifts. Easy in most soils in shade; 8/10.

Melinis

⬍ 60cm/24in

↔ 30cm/12in

✿ late summer–mid-autumn

Z 8

✳ warm

Africa, Asia and Madagascar

A genus of 14 annual and perennial grasses from open ground. Only one is grown in gardens.

M. repens (*Rhynchelytrum repens*)

Grown for its showy intensely pink flowers which float like a haze over and around the leaf mound. Most soils in sun. Short-lived perennial, best treated as an annual; 8/10.

Milium Millet

⬍ 30cm/12in

↔ 15cm/6in

✿ mid-spring–early summer

Z 6

✳ cool

North America and Eurasia

A small genus of annual and perennial grasses from woodland habitats.

Milium effusum 'Aureum' AGM

Bowles' golden grass

One of the gems of spring, this cool-season perennial woodlander forms a loosely tufted plant with soft, limp leaves and slender, open panicles; the plant – leaves, stems and flowers – is yellow, brassy in sun, quieter greenish yellow in shade. It starts into growth in autumn and goes dormant in summer. Easy in most soils in light shade where it will seed itself around gently. Lovely with scillas, bluebells or forget-me-nots, and with pink or red astrantias; 9/10.

Miscanthus sinensis 'Silberfeder'

Miscanthus

Japan, China and Korea, with a few species in Africa

A genus of about 20 large generally robust perennial grasses usually forming tussocks of narrow leaves with erect stems topped by many-fingered plumes whose beauty arises from their ability to catch the sunlight in the hairs and bristles of the spikelets. The stems are solid, unlike those of most grasses. Many species were once included in *Eulalia*, now defined as a tropical genus. They are easily grown in sun in ordinary garden earth. Most take two to three seasons to become established, but may then be left to grow in the same place for many years, even decades. However, since the clumps increase in girth year on year they may eventually become too large for smaller gardens and it may be necessary to reduce their size. They tend to die out in the centre and can be divided to renew their vigour.

The named varieties are propagated by division in spring as leaf growth begins. When propagating from well-established clumps it is best to take material from the outside of the clump where it is growing most vigorously. Often the simplest way is to remove a wedge-shaped piece, like a slice from a round cake. Most varieties of *M. sinensis* produce fertile seed but the seedlings may not resemble the parent. Self-sown seedlings, though interesting, generally detract from the quality of named varieties in the garden.

M. floridulus

↕ 2.4m/8ft

↔ 1m/39in

❊ late summer–early autumn

Z 8

✻ warm

The plant usually grown under this name is now known as *M. x giganteus*. The true plant is a tall-growing species from Japan and the Pacific Islands producing leaves all the way up the stems (not only at ground level) and distinguished from most other Asiatic miscanthus by its elongated rachis, making it look from a distance more like a pampas grass than a miscanthus. The stems are greyish and hairy, and it has a lax, rather untidy habit; 5/10.

M. x giganteus

↕ 3m/10ft

↔ 1m/39in

❊ late summer–early autumn

Z 4

✻ warm

Hybrid between *M. sinensis* and *M. sacchariflorus* 'Purpurascens', grown for its bold broad foliage, which can be used to create a tropical effect. It has thick stems and the upright leaves, which have a clearly defined white midrib, arch away from the stems, hanging downwards attractively. In short growing seasons it may not flower at all; 10/10. **'Gilt Edge'** grows to 2.4m (8ft). Leaves boldly striped and margined old gold. Greg Speikert, of Crystal Palace Perennials, and I spotted this sport on a huge old clump at the self-same second; 9/10. **'Gotember'** reaches 2.4m (8ft). Leaves variously striped and margined bright golden yellow, stems rhubarb red and hairy. In spring the stems are upright, those produced later are oblique. Has a spreading habit; 10/10.

M. nepalensis

↕ 1.5m/5ft

↔ 60cm/24in

❊ midsummer–early autumn

Z 8

✻ warm

Quite distinct from other cultivated miscanthus in its honey-coloured flower plumes, an effect created by the long tawny-coloured hairs on the flowers. Hardiness varies with provenance but generally not as hardy as most. Best increased by division in spring, as seed cannot be relied on. Good for cutting; 10/10.

↕ 1.2m/4ft

↔ 60cm/24in

❋ midsummer–early autumn

Z 7

✽ warm

↕ 1.2m/4ft

↔ 30cm/12in

❋ midsummer–early autumn

Z 7

✽ warm

↕ 1.2m/4ft

↔ 1m/39in

❋ midsummer–mid-autumn

Z 7

✽ warm

↕ 2.4m/8ft

↔ 1m/39in

❋ midsummer–mid-autumn

Z 7

✽ warm

M. x oligonensis

A hybrid resulting from crosses between *M. sinensis* and *M. oligostachyus*, looking like medium-sized forms of *M. sinensis* but with pinker, chunkier plumes. Better known in continental Europe than in Britain; 6/10. **'Juli'** is so named because it is normally in flower in July; 7/10. **'Wetterfahne'** (weather vane) has broad leaves which turn reddish in early winter; 7/10. **'Zwergelefant'** (little elephant) is taller, to 1.8m (6ft) and notably free-flowering with broad, deep green leaves with a well-defined white midrib. The fingers of the flowers get caught in the flag leaf and emerge wrinkled as if treated with goffering tongs, tawny yellow at first becoming strongly pink-tinted; 10/10.

M. oligostachyus

A compact species that is good for cutting, from the mountains of Japan, always smaller in growth and more lightly built than *M. sinensis*. Flower plumes have fewer fingers, usually two or three but sometimes up to five, creating a much less full and fluffy effect. Leaves thinner than those of *M. sinensis* often assuming burnt-red autumn colours. Tolerant of shade and of more cold than *M. sinensis*. The miscanthus known as 'Purpurascens' may belong here. Several variegated forms are cultivated in Japan but only one seems to be known in the West. **'Nanus Variegatus'** (*M. tinctorius* 'Nanus Variegatus') usually grows to no more than 75cm/30in and is one of the smallest cultivated miscanthus, useful at the fronts of borders. Quietly variegated, the short, tapering leaves are irregularly striped creamy yellow, the amount of variegation differ from leaf to leaf, turning yellow in autumn. Produces elegant copper-coloured plumes. The shallow, slowly spreading rootstock is seldom a problem; 7/10.

M. 'Purpurascens'

This is a compact plant with mid-green leaves that have a distinct reddish tinge to them, even in the spring, the colour intensifying as the year goes by until, in the early autumn, the whole plant becomes incandescent with reds and oranges, while at the same time the panicles billow out startlingly white in contrast; later the leaves fade to a burnt ochre while the panicles turn a fluffy oatmeal; 8/10.

Miscanthus 'Purpurascens'

M. sinensis

The most important of all ornamental grasses, no other species showing such beauty of flower, such diversity of foliage, such richness of autumn and winter colouring, such variation in stature nor remaining ornamental for so long. Modern hybridizing has produced varieties varying in height from 45cm (18in) to 4m (12ft), in the width of the leaves and in flowering earlier or later. There are over 200 named varieties: those featured here are representative. Those grown for their autumn colour usually have narrower, paler, more upright plumes with fewer fingers. All can be cut for indoor decoration.

'Adagio', 1.5m (5ft), has very fine foliage and is consistently good in flower, carrying its plumes well above the leaves; the flowers are tinted red on opening, soon fading to creamy white; 8/10. **'Afrika'**, 90cm (36in), is a low-growing, thin-leaved variety with brilliant autumn colouring. Forms dense clumps, slow to increase; 8/10. **'Arabesque'**, 90cm (36in), is another compact, narrow-leaved selection with silvery plumes; 8/10. **'Blüetenwunder'** (wonderful blooms), 2m/6ft, differs from other varieties in producing its white plumes at staggered heights, creating the impression that the flowers are all round the plant rather than just above it; 9/10. **'China'**, 1.5m (5ft), has narrow, small, olive-green leaves and is remarkable for the intense vinous-red colouring of the long-stemmed plumes on opening and for the good reddish autumn foliage colour. Sometimes confused with 'Ferner Osten' but distinct in its narrower leaves; 10/10.

'Dixieland', 1.5m (5ft), is similar to 'Variegatus' but supposedly smaller. In trials at RHS Wisley it matched 'Variegatus' in almost every respect but in the warm climate of America it is considerably dwarfer; 10/10. **'Etincelle'** (sparkler), 1.5m (5ft), is in effect a zebra-striped version of 'Gracillimus'. Stunning; 10/10. **'Ferner Osten'** (Far East), 1.5m (5ft), is a lovely early-flowering variety forming dense, compact clumps of narrow leaves. The flowers are intensely vinous red with white tips while unfurling, becoming silver later. Similar to 'China' but slightly taller, slightly later flowering and distinct in its broader leaves; 10/10. **'Flamingo'** AGM, 1.5m (5ft), is the one most often asked for in my old nursery and the one that seemed to catch everyone's eye in the garden. It has quite the fluffiest flowers of the *M. sinensis* varieties, the fingers of the flowers, rose-coloured to start with, arch upwards and then droop gracefully. The foliage is narrow and arching and turns orange-gold in autumn; 10/10.

Miscanthus sinensis 'Goldfeder'

'Gewitterwolke' AGM, 1.3m (4½ft), is named for a fancied resemblance of the flowers to a thundercloud: the colouring is vinous purple and silver at the same time. Strongly upright habit of growth. Leaves turn orange in autumn; 10/10. **'Ghana'** AGM, 1.8m (6ft), is one of the varieties grown chiefly for the glories of their autumn foliage. Makes upright clumps with cascading foliage; the leaves are thin, as with most autumn-colouring varieties. The late summer–mid-autumn flowers are held upright well above the leaves and are reddish brown at first, becoming silver; 8/10. **'Giraffe'**, 2.5m (8ft), is a tall and stately zebra grass with broad, well-striped leaves, the transverse bands seeming not to develop the red scorch-marks seen on most zebra grasses. Slow to increase; 10/10. **'Goldfeder'** (gold feather), 2.2m (7ft), is the only yellow-variegated variety to date. A sport of *M. sinensis* 'Silberfeder', it makes an upright clump with arching leaves broadly edged and striped yellow and topped by rather thin, pale flowers late in the season. Slow grower. Needs to be in sun; 9/10. **'Gold und Silber'** (gold and silver) AGM, 1.4m (4½ft), is compact with slightly zebra-striped foliage that turns orange-gold in the autumn. The name comes from the golden anthers, which are conspicuous when seen against the silveriness of the late summer–mid-autumn plumes. Ideal for smaller gardens; 8/10. **'Gracillimus'**, maiden grass, 1.5m (5ft), makes very dense, rounded, rather mushroom-shaped mounds with very narrow dark green leaves giving a slightly untidy appearance because not all the leaves are the same width, but in spite of this it produces a finely textured appearance overall. Seldom flowers in cool climates but in warmer climates produces copper-coloured flowers in late autumn; 8/10. **'Graziella'**, 1.8m (6ft), is one of the earliest Pagel's hybrids to gain popularity, and is beautiful both in leaf and flower. The leaves are narrow with a white midrib and the tall stems are topped by large flower panicles held well above the foliage, silvery at first turning white then beige, the flowers resembling ostrich plumes; 9/10. **'Grosse Fontäne'** (big fountain) AGM, 2.5m (8ft), is a strong-growing selection producing an abundance of broad green leaves with distinct silver midribs and large panicles of gracefully weeping flowers that contain more silver than red. The leaves are very long and form a cascading mound. Outstanding; 10/10.

'Haiku', 2.5m (8ft), is similar to 'Grosse Fontäne' but makes a lower mound. It is a robust cultivar with relatively broad leaves, producing its large, showy flower plumes high above the foliage. The plumes are strongly red-tinted on opening, and the leaves assume reddish colouring in autumn; 9/10. 'Helga Reich', 1.8m (6ft), is a lovely selection with evenly fine leaves forming rounded or mushroom-shaped clumps very much in the manner of 'Gracillimus' and with similar flowers, produced earlier and on taller stems. In cooler climates it is more reliable in its flowering than 'Gracillimus'; 9/10. 'Herman Müssel', 2.2m (7ft), is a very fine selection, only recently introduced. What makes it so excellent is that the rather upright, tawny flowers are carried high above the foliage mound leaving a clear gap between flowers and foliage occupied only by the flower stems. This means that it can be grown at the back of a border or among other plants or grasses with only the flowers showing from late summer–mid-autumn, the foliage hidden by the plants in front; 10/10. 'Hinjo', 1.2m (4ft), is a first-rate dwarf zebra grass producing broad, pale green leaves with broad, biscuit-coloured banding and good flowers held only just above the leaves; 9/10. 'Juli' see M. x oligonensis 'Juli' (page 58).

'Kaskade' AGM, 1.9m (6¼ft), is named for the cascading fingers of the flower plumes, red on opening, becoming pink and silver later, and because it produces a succession of flower plumes rather than a single burst. The leaves are broad with white central midribs; 10/10. 'Kirk Alexander', 2.2m (7ft), is regarded as one of the best zebra grasses in America where the leaves are strongly banded; it is really not a success in Britain where in most summers it scarcely produces any bands at all; 5/10. 'Kleine Fontäne' (little fountain) AGM, 1.5m (5ft), is a dwarf variety bearing narrow leaves with strongly marked white midribs; the leaves turn rich straw yellow in autumn. Earlier flowering than many and producing large plumes for the size of the plant, the fingers of the plumes pendulous, opening red and quickly turning almost white; 10/10. 'Kleine Silberspinne' (little silver spider) AGM, 1.9m (6¼ft), was apparently given its name when quite a young plant – it has been found to grow larger than expected at maturity. Quite different from other selections in that its narrow leaves stand out at right angles to the stems and are carried horizontal to the ground, creating a very neat, tidy plant. The leaves have a strongly marked white midrib and take on straw-yellow and red tints in the autumn. The fingers of the flower plume are held more upright than in other selections, are rose-coloured on opening, turning first silver then buff. They are notably fluffy; 10/10.

'Little Kitten', 45cm (18in), is the dwarfest of the miscanthus forms collected to date on Yakushima Island. It looks like a miniature 'Gracillimus' in leaf but produces its panicles well clear of the very narrow foliage. It is not so free flowering as most M. sinensis selections, but indispensible in the scheme of things for its smallness; 8/10. 'Malepartus', 1.8m (6ft), is widely regarded as the finest of the new hybrids and is the yardstick by which the others are judged. A robust, upright grower, it has broad leaves, well marked with a silvery white midrib, that slowly assume an amazing range of ochrous colours, from clearest butter yellow through shades of ochre to rusty browns that glow in the amber light of autumn. One of the earliest large-growing varieties to flower, the plumes are richly reddish purple at first, going through shades of pink to silver and finally turning biscuit brown, and holding its seeds through the attritions of winter weather; 11/10. **'Morning Light'** AGM, 1.5m (5ft), is in effect a white-margined form of 'Gracillimus'. The extraordinarily narrow leaves are thinly margined white; mature clumps look grey from a distance. Does not flower reliably in Britain, but is regular enough in warmer climates; 10/10. **'Mt. Washington'**, 1.8m (6ft), reliably has the most brilliant autumn colouring of all. Stronger-growing than most autumn-colour varieties, making a taller plant. Similar to 'Graziella' in general appearance. Slow to increase; 10/10.

Miscanthus sinensis 'Morning Light'

'Nippon', 1.2m/4ft, is distinct among the smaller miscanthus in having very narrow, very upright plumes – late summer to mid-autumn. Makes a singularly tidy plant; 8/10. **'Nishidake'**, 2.4m (8ft), is usually the first to flower in northern Germany and is remarkable not so much for the quality of its blooms as for their quantity. Produces an abundance of bright green leaves; 8/10. **'Poseidon'**, 1.8m (6ft), is notable for the sheer size of its panicles, scarcely exceeded by those of any other variety. Leaves light green appearing highly glazed; 8/10. **'Püenktchen'** (little dot), 1.8m (6ft) is a zebra grass that forms very dense, rather upright clumps but is slow to reveal its bands, which are rather sparse even when present. Beautiful pinky coppery plumes are produced with great freedom after a long hot summer; 7/10.

'Rigoletto', 1.5m (5ft), is in effect a dwarf version of 'Variegatus', and similar to 'Dixieland' in stature, but much less vigorous. Ideal for smaller gardens; 8/10. **'Roland'**, 4m (12ft), is probably the largest cultivar to date, magnificent at the back of a border or to draw the eye in a larger landscape. Huge plumes are richly pink-tinted and held high above the leaf mound. Stems splay outwards when in flower, but spring upright and remain erect through winter; 10/10. **'Roterpfeil'** (red arrow), 1.8m (6ft), is the tallest of the *M. sinensis* autumn-colour forms. The flowers are reddish brown to start with, fading to silver and making a lovely contrast with the redness of the autumn leaves; 9/10. **'Rotsilber'** (red-silver), 1.8m (6ft), is notable for the silvery stripe down the centres of the leaves and for its large plumes which are both red and silver, later becoming biege and fluffy. Very free-flowering; 10/10.

Miscanthus sinensis 'Rotsilber'

'Samurai', 1.8m (6ft), is grown more for the brilliant yellow of its autumn foliage than for its rather erect, reddish brown flowers. Upright habit; 7/10. **'Sarabandé'**, 1.8m (6ft), is similar to 'Gracillimus' but is an improvement in that the narrow leaves are all the same width, giving the clumps a much more even texture. The leaves have a greyish cast, quite different in effect from the dark green of maiden grass. Reliably free-flowering; 10/10. **'Septemberrot'** AGM, 2.5m (8ft), flowers later than most and is excellent for extending the season. It is an upright grower with broad leaves with white midribs; the leaves turn coppery yellow in autumn. Upright flowers are held high above the leaf mound, red at first turning to silver; 10/10. **'Silberfeder'** (silver feather) AGM, 2.1m (7ft), Z4, is named for the large, feathery flowers that emerge silver with scarcely a hint of pink. An old variety that flowers freely (from late summer–early autumn) in the cold, short summers of northern Europe; 8/10. **'Silberpfeil'** (silver arrow), 1.8m (6ft), is supposed to differ from 'Variegatus' in its more upright habit; the white-striped leaves of the two varieties are indistinguishable. Often sold as 'Variegatus'; 10/10. **'Silberspinne'** (silver spider) AGM, 1.8m (6ft), is distinct in its narrow leaves, which

Miscanthus sinensis 'Strictus'

are almost straight and stand out obliquely upright from the stems. The panicles are made up of long, spidery fingers, reddish at first, becoming silvery, also obliquely upright; 9/10. **'Silberturm'** (silver tower), 2.8m (9ft), is almost as large as 'Roland' but more upright with large plumes carried high above the leaves. Ideal for the backs of large borders or to draw the eye in larger landscapes; 10/10. **'Sirene'**, 1.5m (5ft), is a small-growing narrow-leaved variety with large flowers that fluff out to a silvery white, floating on the air and moving with the breeze. A favourite among the smaller growers; 10/10. **'Strictus'** AGM, porcupine grass, 1.8m (6ft), is similar to 'Zebrinus' but densely clumping and stiffly upright, thus more effective in the garden; 10/10.

'Tiger Cub', 1.2m (4ft), is usually the first of the zebra grasses to show its stripes, these being cream rather than buff, freely produced on narrow, deep green leaves. Good in flower; 9/10. **'Undine'** AGM, 1.8m (6ft), is similar to 'Graziella' but taller. The coppery pink flower plumes are exceptionally light and airy; 10/10. **'Variegatus'** AGM, 2.1m (7ft), is grown for its brilliantly white-striped foliage. This old cultivar makes a rounded mound, the outer foliage arching over so that the tips touch or almost touch the ground. The flower plumes are strongly red-tinted on opening. A marvellous plant in the garden, landscape or in pots when young; 10/10. **'Wetterfahne'** see *M. x oligonensis* 'Wetterfahne' (p.58). **'Yaku-jima'** is a name which embraces several similar cultivars collected on Yaku Jima Island. All have narrow foliage with a conspicuous white midrib, and most are free-flowering but vary in size from 45cm (18in) to 1.8m (6ft). The best have been given varietal names, see 'Little Kitten' and 'Adagio'. **'Zebrinus'** AGM, 2.4m (8ft), is the original zebra grass, introduced in Victorian times. Makes loose clumps of arching, mid-green leaves transversely banded with irregularly spaced yellow markings. As with all zebra grasses, the banding is dependent on temperature and may not develop on the leaves when they first emerge. In hot summers the bands may develop reddish constrictions which do not detract from their overall garden effectiveness, except in very warm areas. Flower plumes copper at first becoming silver; 9/10. **'Zwergelefant'** see *M. x oligonensis* 'Zwergelefant' (p.58).

M. sinensis var. condensatus

Japanese silver grass

A geographical variant from coastal areas of Japan, differing from *M. sinensis* in its greater stature and in having broader leaves with a silvery cast. The flowers open a burnished coppery red. The variegated varieties listed here originated in Japan and were introduced to the West by staff of the US National Arboretum in Washington, DC. Suitable for cutting; 10/10. **'Cabaret'**, 2.1m (7ft), is a dramatically variegated plant, unique among the eulalia grasses in having central (not marginal) variegation: the wide leaves are white with deep green margins. The coppery red plumes are held well above the foliage in warm-summer climates but may not be produced in cooler climates; 10/10. **'Cosmopolitan'** AGM, 2.4m (8ft), is even more striking and even larger. This is not only the finest of all variegated grasses but an outstanding garden plant in any context. The leaves are remarkably wide, as much as 5cm (2in) across, broadly margined and striped a bright creamy white. The flower plumes are presented well above the leaves and it flowers regularly, even in Britain. Occasional green stems should be cut out; 12/10! **'Cosmo Revert'**, 2.4m (8ft), is the name given to a number of selections that originated as green shoots on 'Cosmopolitan'. All make outstanding garden plants with bold, broad, slightly glossy foliage creating a subtropical ambience: **'Emerald Giant'**, **'Emerald Shadow'** and **'Central Park'** belong here.

M. sinensis var. *condensatus* 'Cabaret'

↕ 2.4m/8ft

↔ 1m/39in

✺ late summer–early autumn

Z 5

✻ warm

↕	1.5m/5ft
↔	90cm/36in
✽	midsummer–mid-autumn
Z	7
🌡❄	warm

↕	1.5m/5ft
↔	90cm/36in
✽	midsummer–mid-autumn
Z	7
🌡❄	warm

↕	90cm/36in
↔	30cm/12in
✽	mid–late summer
Z	4
🌡❄	cool

M. tinctorius 'Nana Variegata' see **M. oligostachyus 'Nanus Variegatus'**.

M. transmorrisonensis

Only introduced from its native Taiwan in 1979, this is similar to the M. *sinensis* Yaku-jima group but the narrow leaves are evergreen in mild gardens and the last to lose their greenness in cold gardens. Flowers carried high above the foliage. Plumes abundantly produced and suitable for cutting; 9/10.

M. yakushimensis

As grown at Kalmthout Arboretum in Belgium and the Savill Gardens in England, this forms a dense tuft of narrow leaves which assume red, yellow, orange and brown autumn tints. The thinly fingered flowers are borne with great freedom. Suitable for cutting. Probably a form of M. *sinensis*; 9/10.

Molinia Moor grass

Eurasia

Genus of two or three Eurasian species, only one of which is cultivated.

M. caerulea

Purple moor grass

Native to acid heaths and moorlands, often an indicator of boggy ground, this and its varieties will thrive in ordinary garden soil in sun or a little shade. Three varieties are grown for their variegated foliage but most are grown for their slender elegant panicles borne on long, thin stems and suitable for cutting. Most assume autumn tints in clear yellows. Differs from other ornamental grasses in that the leaves and stems are deciduous and fall away from the rootstock once touched by hard frosts. With most other genera the leaves and stems stay attached to the rootstock until they decay.

'Carmarthen' is similar to the better known 'Variegata' AGM but differs in its white, not cream variegation and in its narrower, almost black panicles produced on green not cream stems. Oddly, the variegation is less bright than that of 'Variegata'; 9/10. 'Claerwen' is similar to 'Variegata' but is much more subtly variegated and has striking, narrow dark brown almost black spikelets; 8/10. 'Dauerstrahl' is a selection with stiffly upright stems that splay out in their upper half, arching slightly carrying very dark spikelets; 8/10. 'Edith Dudszus' is remarkable for its almost black spikelets, borne on stiffly upright stems on a tightly clumping plant; 10/10. 'Heidebraut' (heather bride) has stiffy erect straw-yellow stems bearing slender panicles of yellow spikelets. Retains its character well into winter; 10/10. 'Moorflamme' is similar to the better known 'Moorhexe' in the colour of the stems and panicles, but differs in the way the stems arch outwards, rather than being erect; 9/10. 'Moorhexe' (moor witch) is slightly shorter than other varieties; the dark flower stems and even darker panicles shoot straight up out of the leaf mound and remain close together all the way to the top; 9/10. 'Rotschopf' differs from all other varieties in its foliage, which is tinted dark red throughout the growing season, becoming more richly coloured in autumn. The flower stems are upright-divergent, and the spikelets dark brown; 9/10. 'Strahlenquelle' (source of rays) is an extraordinary variety in which the flower stems all splay outwards from the centre of the leaf mound. Some people like it; 6/10.

'Variegata' is one of the very best variegated ornamental grasses. The leaves are richly striped cream and green, and turn butter yellow in autumn. The flower stems are cream, turning butter yellow in autumn, and the spikelets dark purplish brown to begin with, quickly fading. Grows in sun or shade, though the flower stems are more lax in shade; 10/10.

↕	2.4m/8ft
↔	90cm/36in
❄	midsummer–early autumn
Z	4
※	cool

M. caerulea subsp. arundinacea (*M. caerulea* subsp. *altissima*)
Tall moor grass
This differs from the purple moor grasses in its greater height, its tall swaying panicles being produced high above the leaf mound and so open and airy that one can see through them to the plants or landscapes beyond. They are essentially cool-climate grasses, and though they flourish in Pennsylvania and Maryland and thence northwards, they are not happy in the heat of North Carolina or states further south.

'Bergfreund' (mountain friend) has large, open panicles of tiny greenish purple spikelets which slowly turn to light brown. The effect is of a cloud of tiny insects hovering high above the leaf mound; 10/10. 'Fontäne' (fountain) is an obvious name for this variety whose slender, elegant stems rise almost vertically and then arch strongly outwards, much like the water in a fountain. Best grown as a specimen since the stems get tangled when grown in drifts; 10/10. 'Karl Foerster' makes good mounds of arching green foliage and produces its broad, pale panicles slightly earlier than other varieties. Most suitable for massing; 9/10. 'Skyracer' is an American selection reputed to be the tallest of the tall moor grasses. The stems are stiffly erect and the panicles quite broad and pale. Makes a useful vertical accent; 9/10. 'Transparent' has gracefully arching stems and long, pale panicles with tiny, dark spikelets. Named for the transparent section between the top of the leaf mound and the bottom of the panicles; 9/10. 'Windzolle' (wind sail) is similar to 'Fontäne' but has heavier panicles that sway with every breeze; 9/10. 'Windspiel' (wind's game) is an American selection with an upright habit. It is supposed to splay out at the top like a fountain and dance with the wind; 8/10. 'Zuneigung' (like lovers embracing) has the largest spikelets and the heaviest panicles in the group – the stems arch outwards under their weight and sway in every breeze. In strong winds the stems twist and entwine like lovers. When sodden with rain or dew they bow down, almost touching the ground, gradually resuming their former stance as they dry. The best of the pendulous varieties. Best as a single specimen as groups tend to get their flower stems tangled; 10/10.

Nassella Needle grass

Americas
About 80 cool-season perennial species. All have panicles made conspicuous by their long-awned spikelets. Several were formerly included in *Stipa*.

Nassella trichotoma

↕	45cm/18in
↔	30cm/12in
❄	late spring–early autumn
Z	7
※	cool

N. trichotoma (*Stipa trichotoma*)
One of the few Andean grasses in cultivation in Europe with extremely fine, bright green arching leaves that make a small mound of almost trailing greenery. The panicles, delicate and diffuse, are borne on crimson stems as thin as silk thread that sprawl over the foliage making a hazy, pinky mauve skirt around the plant. In the midst of this cloud, the little dark dots of incipent seeds hover, like the heads of dragonflies among their shimmering wings. Easy in most soils in sun; 9/10.

Ophiopogon

Japan

Genus of about four species of tufted, evergreen perennials in the lily family. The leaves have a resemblance to those of grasses.

O. planiscapus (green form)

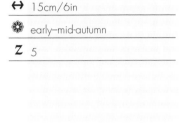

↕ 30cm/12in

↔ 15cm/6in

❋ early–mid-autumn

Z 5

Produces grass-like leaves from a spreading rhizome slowly forming dense, turf-like carpets. The flowers are small, purplish or white borne on short, arching stems. An excellent carpeter; 6/10. **'Nigrescens'** AGM differs in having black leaves. It is the perfect plant for dismal gardens or for black and white gardens, making a startling statement when combined with white-striped sedges, such as *Carex* 'Ice Dance' and *C. morrowii* 'Variegata', or even used to underplant white-striped irises, such as *I. laevigata* 'Variegata' or white- or cream-striped phormiums, including *P. tenax* 'Variegata' or *P. colensoi* 'Tricolor'. Stunning with snowdrops, especialy grey-leaved ones, poking up through it. Also good with *Hemerocallis* 'Sir Blackstem' and *Hosta* 'Little Black Scapes'. Blends easily with plants with dark foliage such as purple heucheras and the darker forms of *Saxifraga fortunei*, with purple cut-leaved maples and so on. Interesting with *Athyrium nipponicum* f. *metallicum* 'Pictum' or 'Silver Falls'; 10/10.

Ophiopogon planiscapus 'Nigrescens'

Oryzopsis Rice grass

Temperate and subtropical regions

Genus of about 20 annual or perennial grasses.

O. miliacea

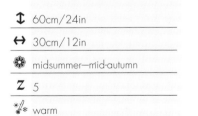

↕ 60cm/24in

↔ 30cm/12in

❋ midsummer–mid-autumn

Z 5

☀/❄ warm

Smilo grass

A fast-growing, drought-tolerant clumper from the Mediterranean, grown in gardens for its decorative panicles, which arch upwards and outwards from the mound of bright shiny green leaves, and then droop, the silky green spikelets swaying at the tips of slender branches; each panicle is as much as 20–30cm (8–12in) long. Matures to golden brown and remains showy well into the winter. Suitable for cutting; 9/10.

Panicum Panic grass

Tropics and cool temperate regions

One of the largest and loveliest grass families with some 500 species of annuals and perennials growing in open ground. Cultivated mainly for their diffuse panicles of gossamer-thin branches and tiny spikelets which create the effect of a cloud of red or mauve insects hovering above the foliage. Indispensable.

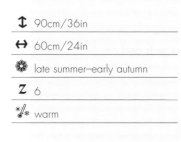

↕	90cm/36in
↔	60cm/24in
❀	late summer–early autumn
Z	6
✳❄	warm

↕	1.2m/4ft
↔	45cm/18in
❀	late summer–early autumn

↕	1.2m/4ft
↔	90cm/36in
❀	midsummer–early autumn
Z	6
✳❄	warm

P. clandestinum

Deer tongue grass

Grown more for its foliage than its flowers; the leaves are very broad for a grass, a rich, lustrous green, gradually turning yellow and russet with unusual purple tints in autumn. In Britain the flowers are borne among the leaves and are scarcely seen, but in the USA they are borne above the leaves in diffuse panicles, silvery at first, brown later; 7/10.

P. miliaceum 'Violaceum'

Purple hog millet

This has about the most eyecatching panicles of any annual grass. They are much-branched, rather like the head of a miscanthus, and green when they come into flower in midsummer but gradually become rich, deep violet-purple. Suitable for cutting. Produces seed most reliably when grown in groups; 8/10.

P. virgatum

Switch grass

A major constituent of the tallgrass prairies that once covered much of North America and showing considerable variation, both in stature and in foliage colour and autumn colouring. Essentially clump-forming, it can also spread by rhizomes, though this is not usually a problem. The upright clumps are overtopped by huge open panicles of tiny purplish spikelets creating a haze of colour above the foliage. Easy in most soils, but best in a moist and fertile one. The blue forms need full sun and perfect drainage otherwise they develop yellowtip death, the tips of the leaves turning yellow and then decaying. Good for cutting.

'Blue Tower', tall blue switch grass, 2.5m (8ft), is a relative giant with good blue foliage and large panicles the same colour as the leaves at first, becoming pale biscuit later. Highly recommended as a specimen. A selection from the native population by Greg Speikert of Crystal Palace Perennials, Illinois; 10/10. 'Cloud Nine', 1.8m (6ft), is a robust grower making well-rounded clumps of steely blue arching leaves. The large paler blue panicles are borne only just above the foliage and have straw-yellow branches that contrast well with the leaves. Makes an excellent specimen. Introduced by Bluemount Nurseries; 9/10. 'Dallas Blues', 1.5m (5ft), is the bluest selection, the broad leaves, flower stems and flowers all the same colour to start with. Panicles large and showy, the plant holding itself elegantly upright; 10/10. 'Hänse Herms', 75cm/30in, is similar to 'Rehbraun', but shorter; 8/10. 'Heavy Metal', 1m (39in), forms tight, rather stiff clumps of grey-blue leaves, stems and flowers. The foliage is butter yellow in autumn; 7/10. 'Northwind' is a tall variety, 1.2m/4ft, with a strongly upright habit and large flower panicles. This and 'Strictum' are the ones to use where a vertical accent is needed to draw the eye; 9/10. 'Pathfinder', 90cm/36in, has powder-blue foliage, not quite as intense as that of 'Prairie Sky', and a more relaxed habit and looser panicles. Flops badly when in flower; 7/10. **'Prairie Sky'**, 1.2m (4ft), is quite the best blue among the moderate growers; it holds itself upright until well into flower, when it seems to become more relaxed. Stays upright best in poor, dry soils on sunny sites, otherwise inclined to flop in wet summers; 9/10.

'Red Cloud', 1.7m (5½ft), is a green-leaved cultivar, noted for the redness of its spikelets, those of most green-leaved varieties being purple. It is a little smaller growing than most; 9/10. **'Rehbraun'**, 1m (39in), is a lovely selection with large panicles of dark purplish spikelets and foliage that takes on brilliant reds and oranges in autumn; 9/10. **'Rotbraun'** (red-bronze), 1.2m (4ft), is similar to 'Hänse Herms', but the leaves stay green in autumn, scarcely colouring at all; 8/10. **'Rotstrahlbusch'**, 1.2m (4ft), another green-leaved selection, is taller with good panicles of purplish spikelets and leaves that take on darker autumn tones than most, being claret deepening to blackberry stains towards the tips; 9/10. **'Rubrum'**, red switch grass, is a name applied to almost any selection whose foliage turns red in autumn. Many plants offered under this name are seed-raised and of variable quality. **'Shenandoah'**, 1.2m (4ft), differs from all the other selections in the intensity of its autumn colouring. Basically, it is a green-leaved switch grass but the leaves start to assume vinous reddish and purplish tones almost as soon as they emerge, the colours intensifying as the season draws on, culminating in autumn when the whole plant glows burgundy red. Selected from among 500 seedlings of 'Hänse Hermes' by Hans Simon at his nursery in Germany; 10/10. **'Squaw'**, 1.5m (5ft), is a tall, green-leaved plant with huge panicles of purplish spikelets strongly tinted pink. A big, vigorous grower but inclined to flop when in flower, though this does not necessarily detract from its overall effectiveness. The foliage assumes a certain amount of red autumn colouring. A sister seedling of 'Warrior', raised by Kurt Bluemel at his eponymus nursery in Baldwin, Maryland; 10/10. **'Strictum'**, 1.5m (5ft), is useful in gardens for its narrow, upright habit, reaching as much as 1.8m (6ft) high in the heat of American summers. The foliage is bluish in the USA, but merely on the blue side of green in Britain. In autumn the whole plant turns a clear, vibrant yellow, making a useful contrast with almost all other cultivated varieties, which assume tones of claret or burgundy. The colour gradually mellows to tan for winter; 8/10. **'Warrior'**, 1.8m (6ft), is a vigorous green-leaved variety, similar to 'Squaw' but more upright and less inclined to flop when in flower. It produces huge panicles of very dark spikelets, and assumes a certain amount of yellow autumn colour; 10/10.

Panicum virgatum 'Rubrum'

Panicum virgatum 'Warrior '

P. 'Wood's Variegated' ('Forest Snow')
Unlike other switch grasses in that the leaves and culms emerge pure white, gradually turning green as the temperature rises; each new leaf also emerges white against the prevailing greens so that a mature clump appears to be white on the outside, green in the centre. Seldom flowers. Must be grown in damp shade. Easily increased by Irish cuttings or stem cuttings rooted in water or wet sand; 10/10.

 30cm/12in

 30cm/12in

❋ early–late summer

Z 5

❀ cool

Pennisetum Fountain grass

Tropics, subtropics and warm temperate regions
Genus of about 80 species of annuals and perennials. The botanical name means feather and refers to the bristle-like flowerheads.

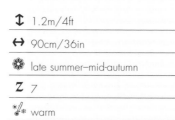

↕ 1.2m/4ft

↔ 90cm/36in

✳ late summer–mid-autumn

Z 7

✳⁄✳ warm

P. alopecuroides (*P. compressum*)

Fountain grass

Forms mounds of green basal foliage from which the flower stems arch upwards and outwards, cascading under the weight of the flowerheads, each like a little, reddish brown fox's brush. Foliage often yellow or sienna in autumn. Easy in any fertile soil and moderately drought-tolerant once established. Good for cutting, but cannot be relied upon to flower well in Britain after grey summers; 10/10. **'Cassian's Choice'**, 90cm (36in), is a selection noted for its brilliant red and yellow autumn foliage colours. The leaves seem to be stained with a hint of amber through the season, and the flowers are a lighter brown than those of the typical plant. Seldom flowers in Britain; 6/10. **'Caudatum'**, white-flowered fountain grass, 1.2m (4ft), has much paler flowers, but nowhere near white; 8/10. **'Hameln'**, 45cm (18in), 36cm (12in), is a dwarf selection that seems to be more reliable in its flowering than some varieties; 10/10. **'Herbstzauber'** (autumn magic), 60cm (24in), 60cm (24in), intermediate in size between the typical wild form and 'Hameln', this flowers slightly later but has larger flowers of a deeper, richer reddish brown; 10/10. var. *japonicum*, Japanese fountain grass, 1.5m (5ft), 1m (39in), is the tallest of the fountain grasses and a vigorous grower; the flowerheads are foxy reddish brown tipped with a little white tuft; 10/10.

'Little Bunny', 30cm (12in), 23cm (9in), is, as one might expect from the name, a mere midget, and useful for that reason if for nothing else. The flowers are typical but smaller, and have somehow lost their charm in acquiring their dwarfness, the flower stems are stiff and do not produce the desired fountain-like effect; 7/10. **'Little Honey'**, 23cm (9in), 15cm (6in), arose as a sport on 'Little Bunny' and has leaves that are longitudinally striped white; 6/10. **'Moudry'**, black-flowering fountain grass, 90cm (36in), 60cm (24in), is most dramatic with smouldering, dusky purplish black flowerheads. A prolific self-seeder in warm gardens; in cool climates seldom flowers at all; 10/10 where it flowers, 2/10 where it doesn't. **'National Arboretum'**, 75cm (30in), 90cm (36in), has the same merits and deficiencies as 'Moudry'; 2/10. **'Paul's Giant'**, 1.5m (5ft), 90cm (36in), is notable for the sheer size of its flowerheads, which are twice as fat and half as long again as with the typical variety, but seems to make up for their size by not producing very many of them. The foliage assumes rich autumnal reds and yellows; 7/10. f. *viridescens*, 90cm (36in), 90cm (36in), is a very leafy form, supposedly with very dark flowers, though I have never seen them, even after growing it for ten years; 2/10. **'Weserbergland'** (River Weser mountain country), 60cm (24in), 60cm (24in), is similar to 'Hameln' but with large, pale flowers borne on longer stems and so producing a more fountain-like effect. Free flowering; 10/10. **'Woodside'**, 60cm (24in), 60cm (24in), was selected by Mervyn Feesey from seedlings in his Woodside garden in Devon and is particularly suitable for English gardens, being reliable in flower, typical in flower form and a deeper in colour, though slightly shorter in stature than the wild type; 10/10.

Pennisetum alopecuroides
'Weserbergland'

P. compressum see **P. alopecuroides**

P. incomptum (*P. flaccidum*)
Meadow fountain grass
Produces dense drifts of greyish green foliage and slender erect, off-white flowerheads rather like bottlebrushes. The **purple** form (*purpureum*) has dusky purple flowers. Aggressive spreaders, ideal for meadows or the edge of woodland or a wild patch, but not safe in a well-manicured garden. Good for cutting; 8/10.

P. macrostachyum 'Burgundy Giant'
A stunning perennial grass with foliage of the richest burgundy red. The broad leaves, somewhat glossy and arching, are topped in late summer with great big furry, arching flowerheads a little lighter in colour than the foliage. Very tender: it needs a minimum winter temperature of 4°C (40°F). Readily propagated by stem cuttings rooted in sand under mist, or less easily in sand with bottom heat. It reaches its full height and flowers in a single season. Good for cutting; 10/10.

P. macruorum
One of the few South African grasses grown in British gardens, this produces a cascading mound of mid-green foliage, above which upright stems are topped with long, pencil-thin, chaffy panicles that are nearly white and, being almost at eye level, draw the eye more strongly than most. It is sometimes confused with *P. incomptum* but differs in its greater height, its coarser foliage and in that it forms clumps that send out runners to form another clump, rather than simply spreading in all directions at the same time. Easily raised from seed and usually flowers in the first year. Easy in sun in good soil. Good for cutting; 10/10.

P. massaicum 'Red Buttons'
Relatively new to cultivation and not yet fully tested for hardiness, this produces quite short, bright red bottlebrushes. The intensity of the colour is unexpected in a grass. Suitable for cutting; 8/10.

P. orientale AGM
Oriental fountain grass
One of the most delightful of all ornamental grasses, one of the longest to flower and one of the most easily accommodated. It forms tufts of soft, arching, grey-green leaves, above which are borne the soft panicles like long, thin bottlebrushes in a subtle shade of mauvish pink – a shade that goes beautifully with the wispy flower spikes of *Aloysia chamaedrifolia* and with the various shades of *Perovskia*. In southern England and the cooler zones of the USA, it starts to flower at midsummer and continues until the frosts, but in warmer zones it may flower as early as mid-spring and still go on until the frosts; 10/10. 'Karley Rose', 70cm (28in), is a patented plant with the richest pink flower colour of all the oriental fountain grasses; 10/10. 'Pakistan' is apparently a white form. It sounds delectable, though I have not seen it. 'Robusta', 90cm (36in), is similar to the typical plant but much taller and with greyer leaves. The flowers are the same colour, but the panicles are longer; 10/10. 'Shogun', 90cm (36in), differs from other selections in its browner flowers; 9/10. 'Tall Tails', 1m (39in), produces long, gently curving heads of pale greenish white flowers with a hint of biege, at the tops of tall, straight stems. Greyish foliage; 10/10.

↕ 1.2m/4ft
↔ 90cm/36in
✳ late summer–mid-autumn
Z 6
⚘ warm

↕ 1.8m/6ft
↔ 90cm/36in
✳ late summer–mid-autumn
Z 10
⚘ warm

↕ 1.8m/6ft
↔ 90cm/36in
✳ midsummer–early autumn
Z 7
⚘ warm

↕ 60cm/24in
↔ 30cm/12in
✳ early–late summer
Z 7
⚘ warm

Pennisetum orientale

↕ 45cm/18in
↔ 30cm/12in
✳ midsummer–early autumn
Z 7
⚘ warm

↕ 1.5m/5ft

↔ 60cm/24in

✳ midsummer–mid-autumn

Z 9

✳ warm

P. setaceum (P. rueppellii) AGM

Tender fountain grass, annual fountain grass

The queen, even empress, of fountain grasses, with long, slender purplish pink flowers with long silky bristles. The flowers can reach 38cm (15in) in length and are lovely for picking and drying. Later flowering than other pennisetums and needs to be started under glass early to ensure a long enough growing season. Easy from seed but named forms need to be raised from divisions. The best plan is to cut down plants to 5cm (2in) in autumn before the frosts; split the clumps, putting small, rooted divisions into cellular trays in a sandy, free-draining mix and overwinter them in a heated greenhouse with a minimum temperature of 4°C (40°F) and good light. Plants will be strong enough to set out once frosts are over; 10/10. The following are grown for their foliage. **'Burgundy Blaze'** ('Rubrum Dwarf'), 60cm/24in, 30cm/12in, differs from 'Rubrum' only in its shorter stature; 10/10. **'Eaton Canyon'** ('Cupreum Compactum', 'Rubrum Dwarf'), 75cm (30in), 30cm (12in), is similar to 'Rubrum' though the leaves are narrower and the colouring is less intense; 10/10. **'Rubrum'** ('Atrosanguineum', 'Cupreum', 'Purpureum'), purple fountain grass, 1.5m (5ft), 30cm (12in), is a rich, glowing burgundy red all over, with broad leaves and silken bristles to the flowers; 10/10.

The red-leaved varieties are all as tender as the green-leaved plant and should be treated similarly. For those who like sharp contrasts, they can look vibrantly exciting planted with the bright blue *Elymus hispidus*, *Mertensia maritima* or *Cerinthe glabra* 'Kiwi Blue'; for those who prefer subtler tones and harmonies, they mix well with other dark-leaved plants such as *Ricinus communis* 'Gibsonii', *Atriplex hortensis* var. *rubra* (purple orach) or *Lysimachia ciliata* 'Firecracker' and, of course, with *Imperata cylindrica* 'Rubra'. They will also look good with dark-leaved plants with sultry flowers such as *Lobelia cardinalis* and *Dahlia* 'Bishop of Llandaff' or the sumptuous *D.* 'Blaisdon Red', or simply combine them with plants with strongly red flowers of the same season, such as *Monarda* 'Mrs Perry' or *Crocosmia* 'Lucifer', perhaps gingered up with the slender soft orange pokers of the small, late-flowering *Kniphofia triangularis*.

↕ 60cm/24in

↔ 60cm/24in

✳ midsummer–mid-autumn

Z 7

✳ warm

P. villosum AGM

Ethiopian fountain grass

This short-lived perennial makes sprawling tussocks of greyish green leaves and produces fluffy white bottlebrush flowers. Neither drought-tolerant nor particularly hardy but flowers the first season from seed. Suitable for cutting; 10/10.

Phalaris

Mainly cooler northern hemisphere

About 15 species of annual and perennial grasses.

↕ 1.8m/6ft

↔ 1m/39in

✳ early–midsummer

Z 4

✳ cool

P. arundinacea

Reed canary grass

A rampant grass spreading rapidly in all directions by means of underground runners (1/10), only the variegated forms of **var. *picta*** are grown in gardens. All are easy in most soils and all too easily propagated by division or runners. True cool-season growers, they often become semi-dormant in summer, even completely dormant in warm summer climates. **'Feesey'** is superior to 'Picta' in that the leaves are a brighter

Phalaris arundinacea 'Picta'

↕ 80cm/42in

↔ 23cm/9in

✱ late spring–midsummer

white, tinted pink when first unfurling. Less vigorous; 10/10. 'Luteopicta' has leaves variegated yellow becoming creamy yellow later fading to green; 8/10. 'Picta' ('Elegantissima)' AGM, striped ribbon grass, gardener's garters, has leaves irregularly striped green and white, the white usually predominating but distributed unevenly across the leaf. The flowers are small whitish panicles, of little interest; 7/10. 'Strawberries 'n' Cream' is similar to 'Feesey' but even pinker, and dwarfer; 8/10. 'Streamlined' is taller growing with basically green leaves striped white; 7/10. 'Tricolor' is similar to 'Feesey' but pinker; 9/10.

P. canariensis
Canary grass, birdseed grass
Widely grown for birdseed, this annual grass has naturalized itself in some of the warmer parts of the world and can be seen as an escape on rubbish tips, even in cool climates like that of Britain. It is grown for its short, fat flowerheads, which are perhaps more decorative picked than in the garden; 5/10.

Phragmites
Worldwide
Genus of four reed species found in wet ground. All spread vigorously at the roots and are very similar to each other. Seldom grown in gardens but the variegated forms are less invasive than the green-leaved ones.

↕ 2.4m/8ft

↔ 1m/39in

✱ early–late autumn

Z 5

❄✱ cool

P. australis (*P. communis*)
Common reed
A very large moisture-loving grass forming extensive communities at the water's edge and only suitable for very large gardens. Variable in stature and flower colour. The stems are widely used for thatching; 8/10. 'Variegatus' forms loose clumps of upright stems bearing tapering leaves, richly variegated old gold. Large, loose, reddish panicles. Happy in ordinary earth where it does not grow so tall nor run so vigorously as the green-leaved form though still needs controlling; 9/10.

↕ 1.2m/4ft,

↔ 1m/39in

✱ early–late autumn

Z 5

❄✱ warm

P. karka
Similar to *P. australis* and often mistaken for it. Differs in its narrower leaves. These two varieties will grow in ordinary earth but are more vigorous in water. 'Candy Stripe' differs from *P. australis* 'Variegatus' in its white-striped leaves, strongly pink-tinted in cool weather; 10/10. Introduced and named by Greg Speikert of Crystal Palace Perennials, Illinois. 'Variegatus' is similar or the same; 9/10.

↕ 1.5m/5ft

↔ 1m/39in

✱ midsummer–early autumn

Z 6

❄✱ warm

P. schezuan
A lovely introduction from Greg Speikert of Crystal Palace Perennials, with a dwarfer habit than other sorts, narrow grey-green leaves and showy pink plumes. Does not run so freely as the other species. Easy in any ordinary garden soil but will grow larger in wet ground. Suitable for cutting; 8/10.

Phyllostachys

Lowland China

About 80 large bamboos, distinguished by the deep sulcus (groove) between the nodes, which is noticeable also on the main branches and rhizomes. Statuesque rather than pretty, all are easy to grow in most soils but must never be allowed to dry out. They appreciate shelter from wind. Classed as runners, they can cover large areas in warm climates; in cooler climates their running capacity seems somewhat suppressed, though they may start running after some years. In smaller gardens, contain the root system using proprietary root barriers of the sort designed to prevent the roots of street trees from spreading. All can be increased by division, preferably in spring.

P. aurea AGM

Golden bamboo

↕ 8m/26ft x 4cm/1½in
↔ 1.8m/6ft in 10 years
z 6

Named for the golden colour the leaves and canes assume in strong sunlight. In less intense sunlight the leaves and canes are green, but the canes are distinct in that the lower internodes are short and the nodes swollen so that the bottom of the cane looks as though it has been compressed from above. Useful for the upright growth of the canes which are well clothed with leaves quite low down, making it an excellent bamboo for hedging or screening. 'Holochrysa' has brilliantly golden-yellow canes. 'Koi' has dull yellow canes with deep green sulca (grooves). Best grown in light shade otherwise the sulcus colour loses its intensity. All 10/10.

P. aureosulcata

↕ 8m/26ft x 3.5cm/1½in
↔ 2.4m/8ft in 10 years
z 6

Quite different from *P. aurea* in its more slender canes, which have a tendency to zig-zag in the lower half. Typically, the canes are green and rough to the touch, with yellow sulca. More cold-tolerant than *P. bambusoides* and should be grown where that will not succeed. A runner in warm climates, but seldom a problem in cold gardens; 8/10. var. *aureocaulis* AGM has golden-yellow canes without any green; 9/10. var. *spectabilis* AGM has golden-yellow canes with green sulca; 10/10.

P. bambusoides

↕ 22m/72ft x 15cm/6in
↔ 3m/10ft in 10 years
z 7

Cultivated in the East time out of mind for its giant canes which can supply a multitude of uses. Forms large clumps of well-spaced thick canes and is distinct from other bamboos in its remarkably long branches. Essentially a plant of the tropics and subtropics, it grows best where summers are warm; 9/10. The varieties have some of the most colourful canes of all bamboos. 'Castilloni' has yellow canes with green sulca and lightly white-streaked leaves. Not so tall as the typical plant; 10/10. 'Castilloni Inversa' has green canes with yellow sulca. Leaves lightly white-streaked; 10/10. 'Holochrysa' ('Allgold') has rich golden-yellow canes; 10/10.

P. bissetii

↕ 7m/23ft x 2.3cm/1in
↔ 6m/18ft in 10 years
z 5

Useful rather than beautiful, this is the best bamboo for hedging and screening, its leaves remaining a clean dark green through the worst of winter weather. Not so tall as many, it is vigorous, forming a dense, leafy canopy that will suppress almost anything else that tries to grow beneath it; 8/10.

↕ 3m/10ft x 5cm/2in

↔ 1.8m/6ft in 10 years

z 7

P. nigra AGM
Black bamboo
The legendary black bamboo with canes green at first, turning black in their second or third year. Initially upright, later arching under the weight of the foliage. It can form large colonies in warm climates; in cooler areas it can be easily controlled. It is one of the best bamboos for container growing. Needs good light to develop its colouring, but too much sun causes the canes to develop unsightly white blotches; 10/10. 'Boryana', 4m (12ft), is a vigorous bamboo producing groves of arching canes that sway in the wind and bear an abundance of small, deep green leaves. The canes are green at first but mature to yellow with purple splashes. Both this and f. *henonis* make excellent specimens on a lawn; 9/10. f. *henonis* AGM, 4m (12ft), is similar to 'Boryana' but the canes are more upright, green at first maturing to yellowish brown. Leaves dark green and shiny; 9/10. f. *punctata*, 3.5m (11ft), is sometimes sold as *P. nigra* but is distinct in that its green canes are mottled black but are never wholly black; 9/10.

↕ 5m/15ft x 9.5cm/3in

↔ 4m/12ft

z 7

P. vivax
Fast-growing and cold-tolerant, this may be distinguished from *P. bambusoides* by its drooping leaves and thinner canes, which are rich deep green. Bears copious foliage causing the canes to arch elegantly. The canes are thin-walled and easily split or broken by wind or snow; 7/10. f. *aureocaulis* AGM is a stunning selection with rich golden-yellow canes with occasional, irregular thin green stripes turning red in strong sunlight. Again, the canes are brittle; 8/10.

Phyllostachys vivax f. *aureocaulis*

*Pleioblastus
argenteostriatus* 'Akebono'

Pleioblastus
China and Japan
A genus of about 20 generally small to medium-sized bamboos. Several are decorative. All are invasive and should never be admitted to small gardens.

↕ 30cm/12in x 5mm/¼in

↔ 90cm/36in

z 7

P. argenteostriatus 'Akebono'
New leaves are wholly white, slowly becoming green at the base, the green eventually suffusing the whole of the leaf. Leaves stay whitest longest in cool shade, but even then turn green by late summer. Easy but must have almost total shade. The least invasive of the genus; 8/10.

↕ 1.5m/5ft x 7mm/¼in

↔ 1.5m/5ft in 10 years

z 5

P. variegatus AGM (*P. fortunei*)
Forms dense mounds of creamy white-and-green-striped leaves, borne abundantly on short, erect canes. Easy in most soils in sun or shade, good in containers. The best foliage is produced if the whole clump is cut down at the end of each winter. 'Tsuboii' (*P. shibuyanus* 'Tsuboii') is taller, 1.8m (6ft), and has leaves variegated with both broad and narrow stripes of green and cream. The young, leafless canes stand erect but later bow down under the weight of the leaves. Runs at the roots but seldom enough to be a problem; both 10/10.

↕ 1.5m/5ft × 3.5mm/⅛in

↔ 1.8m/6ft in 10 years

Z 5

P. viridistriatus AGM (*P. auricomis*)
Grown for its leaves which are richest golden yellow with thin green stripes and borne in great abundance. Needs sun to achieve the brightest colouring, but is a subtler lime green in shade. The new leaves produce the brightest colouring, especially when the old canes have been cut down. By midsummer they have become greener, but if the canes are cut down again a new flush will be produced. The thin canes grow close together and form slowly spreading thickets that are seldom a problem to control. Excellent in containers. Looks well with yellow daisies, such as *Rudbeckia fulgida*, and mauve daisies, such as *Aster* x *frikartii* varieties; 10/10. **var.** *chrysophyllus* has leaves of solid yellow with no green stripes. Needs some shade and not so vigorous as the type; 8/10.

Polypogon
Warm temperate regions
Genus of about 20 annual and perennial grasses.

↕ 60cm/24in

↔ 15cm/6in

✢ early–late summer

P. monspeliensis
Annual beard grass, beard grass, rabbit's foot grass
A slender tufted annual producing showy, very fluffy, almost ovoid flowerheads up to 8cm (3in) long. The minute flowers are almost completely hidden by the long silky bristles that give the flowerhead its soft, fluffy appearance. It is green to start with, but fades to palest beige as the seeds ripen. Naturalized in North America and seeds around lightly in many gardens; 8/10.

Pseudosasa
China, Japan and Taiwan
A genus of six bamboos with long-persisting cane sheaths, usually single branches, and generally smaller leaves than those of other similar genera. They are usually upright growing, and though classed as runners, are seldom a problem in cool climate gardens.

↕ 3m/10ft × 1.5cm/½in

↔ 1.8m/6ft

Z 7

P. japonica AGM
More useful than beautiful, this is excellent for hedging and screening. Distinct from other bamboos in that the two different tones on the backs of the leaves are divided one-third to two-thirds, whereas on all other bamboos with two-tone leaves the two tones are equally divided by the midrib. Forms imposing clumps of upright canes with long-persisting, parchment-coloured bracts and quite large dark green leaves; 7/10. 'Akebonosuji' has leaves boldly variegated creamy yellow. Some branches produce leaves that are entirely cream, others leaves that are entirely green. Overall it is a most colourful bamboo, having everything except elegance; 10/10.

Rhychelytrum repens see *Melinis repens* (page 56)

Rhynchorspora

Warm regions

Some 200 perennials mainly from damp or wet places. Two species are sometimes grown. Both need damp or wet soil and can be grown at the pond's edge with no more than 5cm (2in) of water over the crown. They spread by rhizomes and are easily increased by division. Used to be included in *Dichromena*.

↕ 50cm/20in
↔ 60cm/24in
❋ midsummer–early autumn
Z 8

R. colorata

White-top sedge

Sedge-like plants producing small, spherical flowers at the tips of slim, upright stems, the flowers having a showy collar of five to seven slender white bracts, usually of differing lengths. The main flush of flowers is in midsummer, but in warm regions it will often flower into the winter; 9/10.

↕ 80cm/32in
↔ 60cm/24in
❋ midsummer–early autumn
Z 8

R. latifolia

White-top sedge

Slightly taller and showier than *R. colorata*, producing six to ten white bracts of differing lengths. Flowers produced in summer and then intermittently until winter; 9/10.

Saccharum Sugar cane

Tropics, subtropics and warm temperate regions

Some 40 species of perennial grasses, mostly from moist ground. The genus now includes all those species which were at one time placed in *Erianthus*.

↕ 4.2m/14ft
↔ 1m/39in
❋ early–mid-autumn
Z 6
✳ warm

S. ravennae (*Erianthus ravennae*)

Ravenna grass

The flowering panicles of this species are similar to pampas grass but longer and narrower, tinted pink on opening, quickly fading to silver. In autumn the whole plant moves through shades of orange, tan and purple to subtler tones of beige and brown. In hot-summer climates it is as spectacular as pampas grass but in southern England it is a miserable-looking thing, occasionally producing a bedraggled flower spike that usually breaks in the wind, while further north it is not even frost hardy; 10/10 in hot summer climates, 2/10 elsewhere.

Sasa

Japan, Korea, China

About 40 small or medium bamboos all with invasive roots. The canes emerge horizontally and curve until vertical. Easy in almost any soil, but slow to establish, which can give the impression that they are not going to run – but they all do, and to such an extent that they are really not suitable for gardens or even woodland. They can swamp almost all other vegetation and even obstruct the growth of trees. Nor are they safe in pots since the roots will escape through drainage holes and rapidly colonize any ground beneath. Any weedkiller that will kill grass will kill bamboo – eventually!

↕ 2.5m/8ft x 7mm/¼in
↔ 6m/20ft in 10 years
Z 7

S. kurilensis 'Shima-shimofuri'

Leaves uniquely variegated with myriad fine white lines like pinstripes. Best in shade; 10/10.

↕ Canes 2.5m/8ft x 1cm/½in
↔ 6m/20ft in 10 years
Z 5

S. palmata f. nebulosa

A rampant species with large leaves giving a tropical appearance, distinguished from other species by the brown markings on mature canes. The leaves characteristically scorch at the edges in winter, causing them to look variegated; 8/10.

↕ 1.2m/4ft x 5mm/¼in
↔ 3m/10ft in 10 years
Z 5

S. veitchii

A relatively dwarf species often seen as a low groundcover in woodland. It is distinct from other species in its purplish canes, and wide boat-shaped leaves which wither at the margins at the onset of winter. **f.** *minor* ('Nana') is a dwarf form, to half the height, with leaves which wither even more conspicuously at the leaf margins. Both 10/10.

Schizachyrium Little bluestem

North America

A genus of only one species, separated from *Andropogon* by some details of the flower.

S. scoparium

Little bluestem

↕ 1.2m/4ft
↔ 30cm/12in
✿ late summmer–mid-autumn
Z 4
 warm

Native to the once vast North American prairies; little bluestem varies greatly in stature and habit – some are erect, some floppy – and in the summer colour of its narrow leaves, some forms being bright green, while the forms grown in gardens are mostly blue-leaved selections from wild populations. The leaves and stems gradually become flushed with rich, deep purples, later touched with tints of red and flaming orange. By winter the entire plant is a burnished coppery brown or tan. The panicles, which are the same colour as the foliage, are composed of small, hairy, violet spikelets that quickly turn silvery white and have an amazing ability to catch and hold the luminosity of the sky. They remain in good heart right through winter. Easy in most soils in sun, and benefits from being cut down at the end of winter; 10/10. 'Aldous' is a seed cultivar that is said to have the best blue colouring; 10/10. 'Blaze' is another seed cultivar, said to have the brightest autumn colouring; 10/10. 'The Blues' is a clonal selection from Kurt Bluemel's eponymous nursery with intensely blue leaves and stems. It is hairier than other forms and seems to be less easy to grow; 8/10.

Schoenoplectus
Distributed worldwide

A genus of about 80 annual and perennial plants in the sedge family, all natives of watery or wet habitats.

↕ 1.5m/5ft

↔ 1m/40in

✸ late spring–midsummer

Z 5

S. lacustris subsp. tabernaemontani (*Scirpus tabernaemontani*, *Scirpus validus*, *Scirpus lacustris*) Bulrush, clubrush

Forms clumps of upright, cylindrical leafless stems that carry out the function of photosynthesis and produce little tufts of brown flowers about two-thirds of the way up. The linearity of their stems contrasts well with the roundness of waterlily pads. Prefers wet acid soils and is best standing in water; 7/10. 'Albescens' has nearly white stems with occasional thin green lines; 10/10. 'Golden Spears' has stems that are golden yellow in spring, slowly turning green; 9/10. 'Zebrinus' has dark green stems transversely banded creamy white; 10/10.

Semiarundinaria
Far East

Thought to be a generic cross with *Phyllostachys* and *Pleioblastus* as the putative parents, and possesses the characteristics of both. It is a genus of mainly stiffly upright bamboos with running root systems, useful for hedging and screening.

↕ 7m/22ft x 4cm/1½in

↔ 3m/10ft in 10 years

Z 7

S. fastuosa AGM

Forms tall, dense clumps of upright, deep glossy green canes that age to brownish purple and although technically a runner can remain as a fairly compact clump. Tends to throw out occasional underground stems that start a new clump at their tips; 8/10. var. *viridis* has green canes that do not age to purple. If anything it is even better than the typical form; 10/10.

↕ 7m/23ft x 1.3cm/½in

↔ 3m/10ft

Z 7

S. yaskadake

Another upright species, this differs from *S. fastuosa* in its slender canes and in that it is much more leafy; the leaves are dark green; 8/10. 'Kimmei' has brilliant golden-yellow canes and smaller leaves. One of the few bamboos with golden canes that is not a *Phyllostachys* and valuable for that reason; 10/10.

Sesleria Moor grass
Eurasia

About 30 clump-forming perennial grasses with evergreen or semi-evergreen leaves. While not in the first rank of ornamental grasses, they are useful groundcovers in sun or light shade and are tolerant of drought once they are established.

↕ 45cm/18in

↔ 60cm/24in

✸ early–mid-autumn

Z 4

✳ warm

S. autumnalis
Autumn moor grass

Distinct in its curiously yellowish green foliage and by the lateness of its flowering. The panicles, which can be as much as 15cm (6in) long, are fat spikes, almost black at first becoming silvery grey and covered with silky white stamens. Excellent for massing; 7/10.

↕ 15cm/6in

↔ 15cm/6in

✳ late spring–early summer

Z 4

✳ cool

S. caerulea
Blue moor grass

A curious little grass that seems to have had its leaves put on upside-down, the glaucous blue underside of the leaf being on top and creating a two-tone effect. The flowers are little pompoms borne on the tips of short stems. The clumps are dense and weedproof; 7/10.

↕ 75cm/30in

↔ 60cm/24in

✳ mid-spring–early summer

Z 4

✳ cool

S. heufleriana
Blue-green moor grass

Valuable because it is among the first grasses to flower, often in company with snowdrops, crocuses and early daffodils. The flowers are small, almost black but so covered by the pollen sacs as to appear creamy white. The slender flower stems continue to elongate when flowering is finished and eventually droop under the weight of the seeds and fall to the ground at the sides of the plant. The foliage is evergreen, mid-green above and silvery beneath, and it is held in an upright-divergent tuft so that one sees the backs of some of the leaves as well as the tops of others. Easy in most soils in sun. Like *S. autumnalis*, best massed; 7/10.

↕ 1m/39in

↔ 23cm/9in

✳ mid-spring–early summer

Z 4

✳ cool

S. nitida

This is bigger and bluer than the others, making a dense, upright-divergent clump of leaves; these are blue on both surfaces. The panicles are dense little pompoms on the ends of slender stems borne high above the leaf mound; 7/10.

Setaria Annual Setaria, foxtail millet

Tropics, subtropics and warm temperate regions

A genus of a hundred or so annual or perennial grasses.

↕ 60cm/24in

↔ 23cm/9in

✳ late summer–mid-autumn

S. italica 'Macrochaeta'
Annual setaria foxtail millet

The showiest of several annual species with coarse leaves, the stems topped by flowerheads that look like huge, very hairy, vivid green caterpillars; the long bristles often have a purplish tinge. The sheer weight of the inflorescence causes it to droop in a characteristic way. Good for cutting and drying but the caterpillar effect is usually lost during the drying process, since it is most satisfactory to tie the stems together and hang them upside-down in a bundle; 8/10. *S. glauca* is similar but has bluish leaves and red-tinged awns; 9/10.

Shibataea

China and Japan
A genus of three or four very distinct small bamboos from woodlands. Long cultivated in Japan.

↕	1.2m/4ft x 7mm/¼in
↔	90cm/36in in 10 years
Z	6

S. kumasasa

An enchanting small bamboo instantly recognizable by its small stature combined with its broad leaves and very short branches. The leaves look almost oval and are dark green, ageing to yellowish green, borne very densely. Though technically a running bamboo, it runs so little in cool climates that it can be treated as a clumper. Looks best grown in light shade, and in hot climates needs to be protected from the heat of the day. Lovely massed in woodland. In cold areas where the foliage has been damaged by winter frosts, it can be cut to the ground to induce a new flush of canes; 9/10.

Sinarundinaria see Fargesia (page 46)

Sorghastrum

Americas and Africa
Named for its fancied resemblance to *Sorghum*, this is a genus of about 15 annual and perennial grasses.

↕	1.2m/4ft
↔	60cm/24in
✿	late summer–mid-autumn
Z	4
🎋	warm

S. nutans (*S. avenaceum, Chrysopogon avenaceum*)
Indian grass
Once one of the major ingredients of North America's tallgrass prairies (only big bluestem, *Andropogon gerardii*, being more common), this species has a wide distribution and varies considerably in the wild, there being taller and shorter forms, and green, grey and blue populations. Blue-leaved forms tend to be taller than green-leaved forms. All are clump-forming rather upright grasses. The large, dense panicles are produced on stout, stiff, yellow stems, and are coppery tan with long, protruding, rather bristly awns and conspicuous golden-yellow pollen sacs. In autumn the whole plant turns yellow, and then dries to a warm shade of umber. Lovely as specimens or in drifts. Easy to grow in most soils in sun but best in poor soils. Good for cutting; 8/10. 'Indian Steel', 1.2m (4ft), 90cm (36in), is a seed strain with grey foliage; 9/10. 'Sentinel', 1.8m (6ft), 60cm (24in), is a superb selection with the bluest leaves of all and a very narrow, stiffly upright habit; 10/10. 'Sioux Blue', blue-leaved Indian grass, 1.5m (5ft), 75cm (30in), was selected and named by Rick Darke from seedlings of a forage strain evaluated in Longwood Gardens research nursery. Grown not only for its remarkable blueness, but also for its stiff, upright habit. Lovely among rusty-coloured heleniums or dendranthemums, which echo the flower colour, or with Michaelmas daisies; 10/10.

Sorghum Millet

Tropics and subtropics
About 20 robust annual or perennial grasses.

⬍ 2.4m (8ft)

↔ 1m/39in

✽ late summer–mid-autumn

S. bicolor

True millet, great millet
This annual is sometimes grown in bedding schemes for its large exotic-looking foliage. In its native tropics, it is a huge plant, growing to 6m (20ft), but it is still imposing at the 2.4m (8ft) that can be attained in cooler climates. It produces an abundance of lush, rich green foliage, each leaf up to 90cm (3ft) long and 10cm (4in) wide. From among the leaves the panicles appear, rather in the manner of the silks of Indian corn, in white, pink or purple, followed by orange seeds. In cool climates it needs to be sown under glass to give it a long growing season. It makes an interesting neighbour for *S. nigrum*, which grows to much the same height and has dense panicles of large, black seeds. They both look well grown in groups among large, dusky-flowered autumn plants such as *Eupatorium purpureum* (Joe Pye weed), preferably in one of its smaller forms, or among the fading heads of hortensia hydrangeas, the combination sharpened by the addition of several spikes of *Aconitum carmichaelii* in one of its darker forms; 8/10.

Spartina

Americas and Europe and Africa
Genus of about 15 perennial grasses with spreading rhizomes from damp soils in coastal areas. Only one is widely grown.

S. pectinata 'Aureomarginata'

Striped prairie cord grass
Native to wet prairies in North America, this makes large mounds, 1.2m (4ft) tall, of arching, ribbon-like, gold-margined dark green foliage that sways and sighs with the movement of the wind. The panicles are borne high above the foliage and are composed of curious green comb-like spikelets from which hang conspicuous purple anthers; the spikelets later turn reddish brown. The whole plant becomes a glorious yellow in autumn and then settles into a pale biscuit colour for winter. It is at its most vigorous in wet ground where it will run (though not uncontrollably), but it will grow perfectly well in any fertile soil that is not actually dry; 8/10.

⬍ 2.1m/7ft

↔ 1m/39in

✽ mid–late summer

Z 4

✽/✽ warm

Spartina pectinata 'Aureomarginata'

Spodiopogon

Asia

Genus of about 10 perennial grasses. The name refers to the fancied resemblance of the flowers to a grey beard. From the Greek *spodios*, grey and *pogon*, a beard.

↕ 1.2m/4ft
↔ 1m/39in
✿ midsummer–early autumn
Z 4
⚹ warm

S. sibiricus

Makes dense clumps of bamboo-like leaves and stems topped in late summer by panicles that are ovoid in outline, basically grey but covered with small hairs that catch the sunlight attractively when backlit against a dark background. In most years the foliage assumes purplish and claret tones, going rich brown for the winter. It is very frost-hardy and forms upright clumps when grown in sun, but is elegantly lax in shade, where it will flower and colour slightly less well. Suitable for cutting. Almost any soil that is moisture-retentive. Not drought-tolerant; 8/10.

Sporobolus Dropseed

Distributed worldwide

Genus of 100 or more annual and perennial grasses found all around the world. Floriferous grasses, rather in the manner of *Panicum virgatum*, they need well-drained soil in sun. Slow to build up into big clumps but once established reasonably drought-tolerant. Seen to best advantage where the sun can shine through them from behind.

↕ 90cm/36in
↔ 90cm/36in
✿ mid–late summer
Z 5
⚹ warm

S. airoides

Alkali dropseed

This species from the great grass valleys of California forms upright-arching clumps of fine grey-green leaves above which are carried in great pink cloud-like pyramidal panicles, often produced so densely that the foliage almost disappears; the whole plant turns corn yellow later in the season. Good for cutting; 9/10.

↕ 1.2m/4ft
↔ 90cm/36in
✿ midsummer–early autumn
Z 4
⚹ warm

S. heterolepis

Prairie dropseed

One of the most refined of American grasses, this has large, delicate, diffuse panicles borne on slender stems in great clouds high above the foliage. Unusually for a grass, the panicles are strongly scented, some say of coriander, others merely that it is sweet. The foliage is very narrow and bright green, making upright-arching mounds about 60cm (2ft) tall which in the autumn assume yellow and orange tones before the whole plant turns light camel-coloured in winter. Good for picking. Dry, gritty or stony soils in sun; 10/10.

Stipa

Temperate regions

Once a large genus encompassing many and diverse grasses, including a number of highly decorative sun-loving, clump-forming perennial grasses that require good drainage to flourish. Most have long awns which capture the sunlight. Increase by seed or division. Some species are often included in *Achnatherum* because they share the characteristic of having numerous long awns attached to the flowers giving them a feathery or spiky appearance, or *Nassella*.

S. barbata

Feather grass

Forms low tufts of evergreen leaves and slender, upright flowering stems from the tips of which the silvery awns, up to 20cm (8in) long, stream out and float on the wind; 9/10. 'Écume d'Argent' is a selection with even longer awns – as much as 25cm (10in); 9/10. Both suitable for cutting; the flowerheads shatter soon after flowering, but the individual awns can be used in arrangements.

↕	75cm/30in
↔	60cm/24in
✿	midsummer–early autumn
Z	7
✂	cool

S. calamagrostis

Silver spear grass

Rounded mounds of narrow, arching green foliage above which are borne in abundance, from early summer until the frosts, soft, feathery, greeny white plumes that mature to beige; both green and beige flowers are present most of the summer. Indispensable for mixing with perennials and good for cutting. 'Lemperg' is a compact selection. Both score 10/10.

↕	90cm/36in
↔	60cm/24in
✿	summer–autumn
Z	6
✂	cool

S. capillata

Needle grass

Another stipa with a low mound of foliage and tall, slender stems producing long-awned flowers, but in this case the awns are straight and needle-like, silvery not gold and carried more or less horizontally. Needs good drainage. Suitable for cutting; 9/10. *S. extremiorientalis* and *S. turkestanica* are similar.

↕	90cm/36in
↔	60cm/24in
✿	midsummer–early autumn
Z	6
✂	cool

Stipa calamagrostis

↕	2.4m/8ft
↔	1m/39in
✳	early summer–mid-autumn
Z	7
✴	cool

S. gigantea AGM

Golden oats, Spanish oats, golden oat grass
Not just one of the most beautiful ornamental grasses, but one of the loveliest of all garden plants, remaining in beauty from earliest summer into winter. Forms a low tuft of dark evergreen leaves and slender but robust stems that carry large open heads of individually large, long-awned golden spikelets which dance elegantly in the breeze, high above the leaves. Good for cutting. Best seen in sunshine against a dark background. Dislikes hot, humid climates and will not stand waterlogging in winter; 10/10. **'Gold Fontaene'** is a taller selection with larger, more open panicles of paler golden spikelets; 10/10. **'Pixie'**, 1.2–1.5m (4–5ft), is my own dwarf selection; 8/10.

Stipa gigantea

↕	75cm/30in
↔	60cm/24in
✳	midsummer–early autumn
Z	7
✴	cool

S. pennata

Similar to *S. barbata* but with grey-green, not deep green leaves and marginally longer awns. Good for cutting; 9/10. *S. pulcherrima* is similar.

↕	2.5m/8½ft
↔	1m/39in
✳	midsummer–early autumn
Z	7
✴	cool

S. splendens

Large panicles with long-awned spikelets are held high above the mound of narrow leaves. Good for cutting; 8/10.

Stipa tenuissima

S. tenuissima (*Nassella tenuissima*)

Mexican feather grass, pony-tail grass
A short-lived grass whose stems and leaves are bunched together at the base and splayed out above like the bristles of a shaving brush. The airy panicles start jade-green and turn beige, a succession of fresh panicles being produced until the frosts. Best in poor soil in sun. Seeds itself lightly in most soils. Suitable for cutting. Lovely with almost everything especially in drifts between *Melianthus major* and *Phlomis* such as *P. russelliana* or the pink-purple *P. samia*, or between the yellows of *Rudbeckia fulgida* var. *sullivantii* 'Goldsturm' and the dismal mauves of low Michaelmas daisies such as the *Aster* x *frikartii* varieties, with blue-flowered bearded iris and mauve or magenta alliums. Pony-tail grass is sometimes erroneously listed as a varietal name; 10/10. This should never be confused with *S. tenacissima*, a coarse grass used for paper making.

↕	45cm/18in
↔	30cm/12in
✳	late spring–early autumn
Z	6
✴	cool

Typha Cat-tails, bulrushes

Throughout temperate regions and the tropics

The only genus in its family with 10 or more species, natives of wetland habitats. All spread by stout rhizomes to form dense colonies and are plants of lakes rather than ponds, most being exceedingly invasive. They are distinct from other grasses or grass-like plants in both their leaves and flowers. Their leaves, which are flat and sword-like, are produced in two ranks, rising straight up from the base of the plant and in some species eventually arching outwards; they often turn clear yellow in autumn. The flowers are in two parts, the males are produced at the tops of the stems, the females below them, sometimes with a gap between the two. The female flowers are densely packed to form a cigar-like cylinder around the stem, green at first ripening to nearly black in most species. They last well into winter but eventually shatter to scatter their hair-like seeds to the wind. Those in cultivation are suitable for cutting.

↕ 1.8m/6ft

↔ 60cm/24in

✳ early autumn–early winter

Z 3

T. angustifolia

Dwarf cat-tail

Similar to *T. latifolia* but smaller and more elegant in all its parts. The male and female flowers are separated by a distinct space; 7/10.

↕ 3m/10ft

↔ 1m/39in ―

✳ early autumn–early winter

Z 3

T. latifolia

Common cat-tail, common bulrush

The common cat-tail of ponds and lakes, conspicuous late in the year with its large dark brown flowerheads, the male and female section running together without a gap. Popular for dried flower arrangements. An aggressive colonizer, it is totally unsuitable for small domestic ponds; 7/10. **'Variegata'** has white-striped leaves. It is singularly lacking in vigour so is suitable for small ponds; 8/10.

↕ 75cm/30in

↔ 75cm/30in

✳ late summer–mid-autumn

Z 5

T. minima

Miniature cat-tail

Quite distinct from larger cat-tails in its round, not elongated, female flowers borne immediately below a proportionately short spike of male flowers. Ideal for small domestic ponds, but beware, *T. angustifolia* is often sold under this name; 10/10.

Typha minima

Uncinia Hook sedges

Antipodes

Genus of 40 or so sedges differing from European and Asian sedges in that the tips of the seeds terminate in a bristle that turns backwards to form a hook, which readily catches on clothing or animal hair. They are grown for their coloured foliage and are mostly rather similar. The two listed here are much confused in the trade but may be distinguished by their differing leaf widths. Happiest in cool, moist climates like that of the Pacific Northwest or the UK; unhappy in the hot, dry summers of much of North America and Europe. They mix well with yellow or yellowish foliage and with silverlings.

U. rubra

Forms a loosely tufted clump of narrow red or reddish brown leaves. In effect a smaller version of *U. uncinata*, but distinct in its much narrower leaves and less vigorous habit; 10/10.

↕ 20–25cm/8–10in
↔ 20cm/8in
✳ early–late summer
Z 8

U. uncinata

A vigorous, densely tufted plant with variable foliage colour depending on soil and season, but usually green or reddish in the wild, rich mahogany red in the forms normally grown in gardens. A native of forests, it dislikes exposure to strong sun and wind, yet needs a certain amount of sun or good light to develop its best colouring. Needs rich, moist but well-drained soil. Distinguished from *U. rubra* by its greater vigour and broader leaves; 10/10.

↕ 40cm/16in
↔ 30cm/12in
✳ early–late summer
Z 7

Zea Maize, Indian corn, sweetcorn

Central America

A genus of four species of tall, robust annual grasses.

Z. mays

A large coarse annual varying considerably in stature and grown either for its cobs (corn), which are edible and can be brightly coloured, or for its foliage, which is not only bold, creating a subtropical effect, but also often coloured or variegated. The male flowers, known as tassels, are produced at the top of the plant and resemble flowers of miscanthus, but are much coarser; the female flowers are produced at the side of the main stem about halfway up. Known as silks, they have a mass of long, silky threads protruding from the leafy sheath that encloses the flowers, which later turn into the cobs. Where cobs are wanted, plants are usually set out in groups or blocks, not rows, to facilitate pollination. Many named varieties have come and gone over the years, but the following are worth seeking out. 'Fiesta' has long grains coloured red, yellow, white, blue and purple; 10/10. 'Harlequin' has striped red and green leaves, and red cobs; 10/10. 'Indian Corn' has multicoloured grains; 8/10. 'Quadricolor' has leaves striped white, yellow, pink and green; 10/10. 'Strawberry Corn' has small burgundy grains in yellow husks; 10/10. 'Variegata' ('Albovariegata') has white-striped leaves; 9/10.

↕ 2.4–3.6m/8–12ft
↔ 90cm/36in
✳ late summer–mid-autumn

Practical projects

Adapt these plans to suit conditions in your garden, and its size. In small gardens use one of each plant, in larger ones 3–5 or more. The key is to retain the relationships between the plants. Remember the grasses set the structure of the schemes, but it is colour that creates mood. Change the balance to suit your taste.

SHADE

Shaded sites are the most difficult in which to make effective plantings of ornamental grasses since they are mainly plants of open, sunny sites. However, there are grasses that naturally grow in shaded areas, such as woodland, and by choosing these, together with other plants that are grasses in a looser sense, such as sedges and woodrushes, it is possible to make enchanting, restful schemes that are every bit as attractive as those that can be made in sun. Indeed, this is often a highly successful way to brighten up a dark corner where many other plants will not grow. This border is intended for a shaded position between the walls of a house facing north and east (in the northern hemisphere), but it could easily be adapted to almost any shaded site, even at the edge of woodland. The planting combines early summer interest with colour for late summer and into the winter, and includes a few evergreen or winter-growing plants for continuity. It relies quite heavily on sedges (*Carex*), which can generally be expected to do better in shade than most of the true grasses. The design builds up from its lowest point in the north-east corner to its highest point in the south-west corner, taking the eye from the darkest plant in the scheme up to the most luminous.

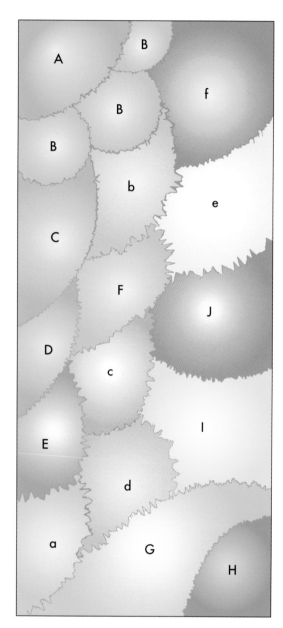

Miscanthus sinensis 'Strictus'

KEY

Grasses

A *Fargesia murielae* or *F. nitida*
B *Miscanthus sinensis* 'Variegatus'; *M. sinensis* 'Zebrinus' or similar
C *Calamagrostis* x *acutiflora* 'Karl Foerster'
D *Miscanthus* 'Purpurascens'
E *Chasmanthium latifolium*
F *Deschampsia cespitosa* 'Goldtau'
G *Carex* 'Ice Dance'
H *Ophiopogon planiscapus* 'Nigrescens'; *O. planiscapus* 'Ebony Knight' is similar
I *Carex comans* 'bronze'
J *Hakonechloa macra* 'Aureola'

Others

a *Adiantum pedatum* or *Sesleria autumnalis*
b *Astilbe* x *arendsii* 'Amethyst'
c *Astrantia* 'Hadspen Blood'
d *Persicaria virginiana* 'Painter's Palette'
e *Hosta* 'Halcyon'
f *Heuchera micrantha* var. *diversifolia* 'Palace Purple'

Most ornamental grasses grow and flower best in an open position, where they are in the sun almost all day. As they will not flower freely without good light, a border of grasses in shade must rely more heavily on foliage effects than on flowers. In the early summer, foliage colour and plant form dominate. The tallest plant is the bamboo *Fargesia murielae* (A), which is virtually evergreen and has light green almost oval leaves and a rounded, weeping habit; it moves gracefully in the wind. The bamboo is surrounded on three sides by the brightly white-variegated grass *Miscanthus sinensis* 'Variegatus' (B), which in shade makes round mounds of rather lax foliage. Its luminosity is echoed at the opposite corner of the scheme by the white-edged *Carex* 'Ice Dance' (G). A second theme in the planting is dark or bronze foliage, announced by *Ophiopogon planiscapus* 'Nigrescens' (H) in the north-east corner and taken up by copper-leaved *Carex comans* 'bronze' (I) and *Heuchera micrantha* var. *diversifolia* 'Palace Purple' (f). The two themes are drawn together in *Persicaria virginiana* 'Painter's Palette' (d) – its cream-coloured leaves are decorated with inverted mahogany

Luzula sylvatica 'Taggart's Cream' (above) *Calamagrostis* x *acutiflora* 'Karl Foerster'.

chevrons. The rich golden colouring of golden hakone grass, *Hakonechloa macra* 'Aureola' (J) adds warmth to the scheme and forms an effective transition between the brightness of the whites and the darkness of the blacks.

The flowering grasses start to perform in late spring or early summer with *Deschampsia cespitosa* 'Goldtau' (F). Above dark, almost evergreen foliage, this compact grass produces misty clouds of tiny acid-yellow spikelets, which turn to the colour of ripe corn and last until winter. The softness of these flowerheads is contrasted with the stiffly erect, pencil-thin plumes of *Calamagrostis* x *acutiflora* 'Karl Foerster' (C), which flowers at the same time and will also remain eyecatching well into winter. They are joined from midsummer by the many-fingered, almost white plumes of *Miscanthus* 'Purpurascens' (D), its foliage slowly taking on tints of vinous purple, and

Alternatives

This scheme is based on the sorts of plants found in indigenous woodland in the English midlands, which is showiest in early summer when red campion, native bluebells and wild garlic all flower together. The few alien grasses are included to provide late summer and winter display.

Grasses

A *Miscanthus* x *giganteus* rustling leaves

B *Miscanthus transmorrisonensis* shiny evergreen leaves

C *Spodiopogon sibiricus* an interesting texture, like a bamboo, and good autumn colouring

D *Calamagrostis brachytricha* for its lateness

E *Hystrix patula* bottlebrush-like pink and green flowerheads

F *Deschampsia cespitosa* 'Goldschleier' greenish yellow panicles

G *Carex plantaginea* broad, plantain-like leaves and white flowers in early spring

H *Luzula sylvatica* 'Taggart's Cream' or 'Marginata' trouble-free and lovely

I *Carex morrowii* 'Variegata' adds texture, the variegation is very slight

J *Millium effusum* 'Aureum' underplanted with Tenby daffodils (*Narcissus obvallaris*), to provide a harmony in yellows

Others

a *Polystichum setiferum* with *Galanthus reginae-olgae* increases the winter effect

b *Allium ursinum* (ramsons, wild garlic) whiteness and fragrance

c *Astrantia major* subsp. *involucrata* 'Shaggy' underplanted with *Galanthus nivalis* 'Flore Pleno' extends the season of interest

d *Silene dioica* (red campion) long flowering season, lovely with bluebells

e *Hyacinthoides non-scripta* (bluebells)

f *Geranium sylvaticum* late flowering

Chasmanthium latifolium (E) with pendulous, locket-like spikelets that seem to have been starched and ironed.

The non-grassy plants in this scheme have been chosen because their leaves produce a sharp contrast to the foliage of the grasses, which is always linear. The leaves of the hostas are sumptuous and heart-shaped, while those of the other plants are made up of a multiplicity of leaflets, perhaps most notably in the fern *Adiantum pedatum* and also in *Astilbe* x *arendsii* 'Amethyst'.

Coping with roots

In shade cast by trees, roots are often a problem, especially if the trees are shallow-rooting, like birches, cherries or beeches, but much less of a problem if they are deep-rooting, like oaks. It is best to avoid planting under shallow-rooting trees. Hedge roots can be kept away from ornamental plantings by using root barriers such as those designed to stop the roots of street trees spreading under pavements.

Food and water

The best way to deal with both the impoverishment of the soil and the competition for moisture that is typical in sites under trees is to mulch the ground in spring and autumn with an organic material such as garden compost or really well-rotted stable or farmyard manure.

Leaves on the ground

Leaf fall can be a problem under trees as the carpet of slowly rotting leaves will suppress new growth. It is best to remove the leaves, stack them to rot and then use them later as a mulch.

Hakonechloa macra 'Aureola' (right), *Deschampsia cespitosa* 'Goldschleier' (below) and *Hystrix patula* (below right).

PRAIRIE

This scheme relies mainly on genuine prairie plants. It is designed to fill the end of a small garden, surrounded on three sides with fencing and seen across a lawn. The plants are all arranged in drifts, as they would be in the prairies. The plan as shown is schematic, indicating the relationship of one plant to another and, as such, it can readily be adapted to other situations. One might simply take the left-hand side of the scheme to use in a long border, or a corner for a corner bed and so on. Prairie plantings have an exceptionally long season of interest, peaking in late summer and autumn, and once planted and established, require relatively little maintenance. Plants should be allowed to seed among themselves to some degree to increase the feeling of naturalness.

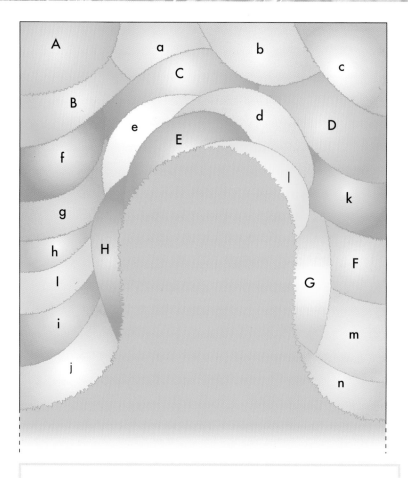

KEY

Grasses

A *Miscanthus sinensis* 'Silberfeder'

B *Panicum virgatum* 'Blue Tower'

C *Sorghastrum nutans* 'Indian Steel'

D *Andropogon gerardii*

E *Deschampsia cespitosa* 'Goldtau'

F *Panicum virgatum* 'Dallas Blues'

G *Sporobolus heterolepis*

H *Schizachyrium scoparium*

I *Pennisetum alopecuroides* 'Hameln'

Others

a *Aster* 'Climax'

b *Eupatorium purpureum* subsp. *maculatum* 'Gateway'

c *Persicaria polymorphum*

d *Perovskia atriplicifolia* 'Blue Spire'

e *Rudbeckia fulgida* var. *sullivantii* 'Goldsturm'

f *Actaea simplex*

g *Gaura lindheimeri* 'Siskiyou Pink'

h *Veronicastrum virginicum* 'Roseum' (*V. virginicum* var. *incarnatum*)

i *Aster x frikartii* 'Mönch'

j *Nepeta x faassenii*

k *Helenium autumnale* 'Moerheim Beauty'

l *Sedum telephium* 'Matrona'

m *Echinacea purpurea*

n *Stachys byzantina*

The prairies, which at one time stretched as far as the eye could see in all directions across the plains of North America, were typically dominated by grasses, especially big bluestem (*Andropogon gerardii*; D), which was once the most common plant in the tall-grass prairie; Indian grass (*Sorghastrum nutans*; C), was the next most dominant, and little bluestem (*Schizachyrium scoparium*; H), switch grass (*Panicum virgatum*; B, F), mosquito grass (*Bouteloua curtipendula*), Canadian lyme grass (*Elymus canadensis*) and prairie dropseed (*Sporobolus heterolepis*; G) were also widespread. Typically, these grasses grew in drifts of single species, the species changing with the habitat. Among them, in smaller numbers, grew plants with showier flowers. Many were daisies great or small, such as Michaelmas daisies (*Aster*), cone flowers (*Echinacea*), black-eyed Susans (*Rudbeckia*), *Heliopsis*, sneezeweed (*Helenium*) and goldenrod (*Solidago*).

Modern garden interpretations of prairies are somewhat stylized and are often enhanced by the addition of, in particular, showy grasses from Asia, such as the highly decorative eulalia grasses (*Miscanthus*; A) and fountain grasses (*Pennisetum*; I) and there are often a few non-prairie perennials that will extend the season.

In any prairie planting, the grasses should dominate but the selection of the perennials is important: they create the

Deschampsia cespitosa 'Goldtau'

Alternatives

The main scheme contains several grasses with blue leaves, flowers and stems, designed to give a sense of distance. In this alternative these have been replaced by green-leaved grasses to produce a richer quality to the colouring. The perennials have also been varied to gain greater depth of colour. The scheme omits the aliens and is composed entirely of genuine prairie plants.

Grasses

A *Elymus canadensis* arching panicles like prickly caterpillars

B *Panicum virgatum* 'Warrior' abundant flowers

C *Sorghastrum nutans* foxy-red panicles

D *Spartina pectinata* 'Aureomarginata' arching foliage

E *Panicum virgatum* 'Shenandoah' vinous-purple summer leaves

F *Bouteloua curtipendula* odd, one-sided panicles

G *Eragrostis spectabilis* huge panicles

H *Bouteloua gracilis* curious pendent spikelets

I *Chasmanthium latifolium* locket-like flowerheads

Others

a *Asclepias tuberosa* brilliant brick-orange flowers

b *Ratibidia columnifera* height and yellow daisies

c *Amorpha fruticosa* purplish blue flowers in high summer

d *Liatris spicata* late spikes of magenta flowers

e *Yucca filamentosa* textural quality

f *Oenothera odorata* primrose flowers opening in the evening

g x *Solidaster* 'Super' pale yellow flowers

h *Baptisia australis* blue flowers and black seeds

i *Aster lateriflorus* 'Horizontalis' showers of light mauve flowers

j *Salvia verticillata* 'Purple Rain' upright spikes of deep purple

k *Solidago speciosa* long season of yellow flowers

l *Echinacea purpurea* 'Kim's Knee High' low stature and pinkish flowers

m *Echinacea pallida* earlier flowering

n *Monarda* 'Mohawk'

Panicum virgatum 'Warrior'

best counterpoint to the grasses when care is taken to choose those with forms of flowers and flowerheads that provide effective contrasts both with the grasses and with each other. It is also possible to include many that have seedheads that remain effective as decoration until late winter. In this design *Sedum telephium* 'Matrona' (l) in the foreground, with its flat heads of richly coloured flowers contrasts well with the thin, whispy blue spikes of *Perovskia atriplicifolia* 'Blue Spire' (d), and both of these contrast with the rounded shapes of the flowerheads of *Eupatorium purpureum* subsp. *maculatum* 'Gateway' (b) behind them. Similarly, the thin pale pink spires of

Beware of Rich Soil

The prairies, like most of the major grasslands of the world, exist on poor soils. By contrast, most garden soils are relatively rich. When the plants from poor soils are planted in rich soils, they grow out of character: they get too big and too lush and consequently have weak stems and tend to flop and fall, to break in wind or rain. They are also prone to diseases from which they are usually free in the wild. However, most garden soils can be made poorer by digging in copious quantities of coarse sand, pea-grit or shingle and by mulching.

Veronicastrum virginicum 'Roseum' (h) create a counterbalance to the horizontal plane of the petals of the cerise daisies of *Echinacea purpurea* (m) and with the delicate pink flowers of *Gaura lindheimeri* 'Siskiyou Pink' (g) floating like butterflies on thin, wiry stems above the others.

Extending the season

Typically, the plants of the prairies are late to start into growth, and later into flower than the traditional flowering plants of the herbaceous border. The season can be brought forward by underplanting the taller growers at the back of the scheme with prairie camas lilies (*Camassia leitchlinii* and *C. cusikii*) in varying shades of blue and occasionally almost white; these are genuine prairie bulbs. Interplant some of the perennials in the same area with stoloniferous prairie lilies such as *Lilium canadense*, *L. michiganense* and *L. superbum*. Plant the foreground with *Geranium tuberosum* whose delicate cut leaves appear through the winter and die away in summer.

Soil type

The best soils for grasses are moisture-retentive and slightly alkaline. Soils can be made moisture-retentive by adding organic materials such as garden compost, coir, leaf-mould, but not farmyard or stable manure. Add lime or limestone powder to increase alkalinity if necessary.

Weeds

In poor soils the plants recommended for this scheme will use up the available moisture and nutrients in the ground, giving weed seeds little encouragement to germinate and become established. However, the scheme will be much more effective if obvious aliens, such as native trees and shrubs, and soft grasses, are removed as they appear.

Maintenance

Provided that they are sited in sun all day on deep, moisture-retentive soil, prairie natives generally make good garden plants, needing little watering and no feeding. They will usually need hand weeding for the first two or three years until established. They should to be well watered in at planting time. After that they should only be watered if they roll their leaves (which are usually flat), a sure sign that they need water.

Since prairie plants are mostly late-summer flowering the season needs to be extended forwards with early flowers like the violas used here.

WATERSIDE

This scheme is for the surroundings of a pond and is intended for a reasonably large garden, the rest of which is not shown. It will work well for a natural pond that has damp soil around it, but can also be used beside an artificial pool, provided that an area of damp soil is created at its edge. The path, which should be of gravel or bark over a hardcore foundation, acts to separate the damp area from ordinary earth, and the planting on the 'ordinary' side reflects this. The planting could be done without the pond, but then the plants actually growing in the water would have to be omitted. The success of the scheme relies on the sun being beyond the planting, and the tallest plants being at the back. So long as this general concept is adhered to, it could work even on uneven ground, providing it is wet enough.

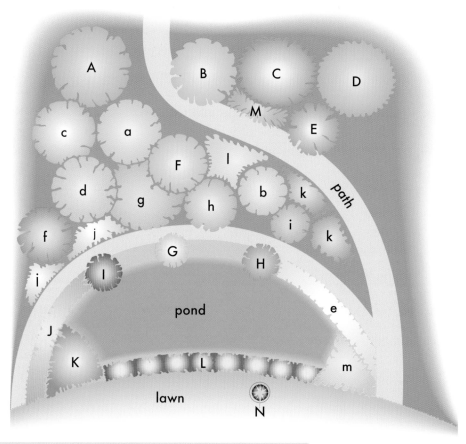

KEY

Grasses

A Arundo donax

B Phyllostachys mannii
or Fargesia murielae

C Miscanthus x giganteus

D Miscanthus sinensis
'Malepartus'

E Miscanthus sinensis 'Zebrinus'
or M. sinensis 'Strictus'

F Spartina pectinata
'Aureomarginata'

G Glyceria maxima 'Variegata'

H Schoenoplectus lacustris subsp.
tabernaemontani 'Zebrinus'

I Schoenoplectus lacustris subsp.
tabernaemontani 'Albescens'

J Carex elata 'Aurea'; 'Sue
Ward' is similar

K Acorus calamus 'Variegatus'

L Eriophorum angustifolium

M Molinia caerulea 'Variegata'

Others

a Aruncus dioicus

b Darmera peltata

c Filipendula rubra 'Venusta'

d Lythrum salicaria

e Zantedeschia aethiopica
'Crowborough'

f Rheum palmatum
'Atrosanguineum'

g Astilbe 'Professor van der
Wielen'

h Ligularia 'Desdemona'

i Iris ensata

j Primula florindae

k Primula japonica

l Matteuccia struthiopteris

m Iris laevigata 'Variegata'

Carex elata 'Aurea' (top) and Glyceria
maxima 'Variegata' (below).

The pond is in the foreground with the planting banked up behind it. Waterside soil and damp ground offer an opportunity to indulge in a few really lush, strong-growing plants that simply will not thrive in ordinary earth. The downside is that the weeds will flourish here too, so it is important to put enough plants in the ground, close enough together, to grow together to crowd out the weeds. The site faces north so the sun rises to the left of the planting and passes over it to set on the right. The essence of the design is that the flowers and foliage are seen against a dark background with the sun behind or beside them, hence the background planting of big grasses – *Arundo donax* (A), *Phyllostachys mannii* (B), which is the best bamboo for wet sites, *Miscanthus* x *giganteus* (C), and *M. sinensis* 'Malepartus' (D).

Creating a damp area

Where the soil is not naturally damp, it can be made so by artificial means. First dig out the ground to a depth of 45cm (18in), creating a hole with sloping sides. Cover the surface of the hollowed-out area with 5cm (2in) of soft sand. Lay a pond liner over the sand. Create a few holes (eight to ten for a small area, more for larger areas). Finally return the soil to fill the liner and plant. The pond liner will impede drainage while the holes will ensure the area doesn't get too wet.

In spring and early summer, this essentially green background provides the backdrop for lighter-leaved plants. Illuminated as if lit from within are the long thin golden leaves of Bowles' golden sedge (*Carex elata* 'Aurea'; J), the large, shaggy leaves of *Rheum palmatum* 'Atrosanguineum' (f) and the pink-, white- and green-striped early foliage of the striped manna grass (*Glyceria maxima* var. 'Variegata'; G), echoed by the similarly coloured leaves of *Acorus calamus* 'Variegatus' (K). The whole is balanced on the other side of the pond by the leaves of *Iris laevigata* 'Variegata' (m), with their green and white stripes. The sword shapes of the leaves of the acorus and the iris are reflected in *Iris ensata* (i).

In midsummer, the cotton grass (*Eriophorum angustifolium*; L) comes into its own, its pristine fluffy seedheads, like hundreds of cotton balls bobbing in the wind, forming a continuous white line across the

Alternatives

This alternative planting scheme is designed to create a far jazzier effect, the foliage of most of the grasses being yellow-variegated while the flowers of the other plants are mainly in bright primary colours. It will work best if the site is in sun, and the plants are well fed.

Grasses

A *Miscanthus sinensis* 'Goldfeder' gold-striped leaves
B *Panicum virgatum* 'Cloud Nine' overall blueness
C *Miscanthus sinensis* 'Zebrinus' gold-banded leaves
D *Phragmites australis* 'Variegata' gold-striped leaves
E *Pleioblastus variegatus* 'Tsuboii' cream variegation
F *Miscanthus sinensis* 'Hinjo' gold-banded leaves
G *Hakonechloa macra* 'Aureola' green and golden leaves
H *Pleioblastus viridistriatus* gold and green leaves
I *Schoenoplectus lacustris* subsp. *tabernaemontani* 'Golden Spear' upright habit and golden stems
J *Bromus inermis* 'Skinner's Gold' golden leaves
K *Cyperus longus* curious flowerheads
L *Eriophorum angustifolium* cotton-like seedheads
M *Carex elata* 'Sue Ward' brilliant yellow leaves

Others

a *Cardiocrinum giganteum* fragrance and imposing stature
b *Iris sibirica* in a light blue shade
c *Lobelia tupa* grey leaves and overall architecture
d *Hemerocallis* 'Hyperion' fragrant yellow trumpet flowers
e *Tropaeolum majus* in its natural orange colour
f *Lobelia syphilitica* vibrant blues
g *Ligularia przewalskii* dramatic spires of yellow daisies
h *Lobelia cardinalis* brilliant scarlet flowers
i *Trollius europaeus* early golden buttercups
j *Primula* 'Inverewe' candlabras of soft orange flowers
k *Persicaria bistorta* 'Superbum' late, pink spires
l *Hosta lancifolia* narrow leaves and deep purple flowers
m *Mimulus guttatus* red-dappled yellow flowers

front of the pond. While across the water, the leaves of the striped manna grass have matured to a rich creamy yellow and green. Later in the summer, the tall flowering plants produce variations on a theme of feathery plumes; rosy pink *Filipendula rubra* 'Venusta' (c), creamy white *Aruncus dioicus* (a) and deep ruby-red *Astilbe* x *arendsii* 'Glut' (glow) (g), are sharpened up by the vivid cerise spires of *Lythrum salicaria* (d), and all are brought alive by the sun's backlighting.

Finally, in the autumn, the major grasses come into full flower: *Miscanthus sinensis* 'Malepartus' (D), *Miscanthus sinensis* 'Zebrinus' (E), as well as *Spartina pectinata* 'Aureomarginata' (F), whose leaves turn shades of butter yellow, ochre and burnt sienna before fading to the buffs and beiges of winter.

Water wise

In times of drought, the water table will fall as will levels in the pond. Since the plants in this scheme are highly water-dependent they will need watering if they show signs of distress.

Bamboo care

Bamboos need little maintenance beyond removing dead or broken canes. Regular mulching with organic materials will keep clumps healthy.

Care

Both *Glyceria maxima* 'Variegata' and *Eriophorum angustifolium* run at the roots and should be cut back to size every winter; the glyceria looks best if it is cut down in midsummer. This prevents it from growing too tall and becoming floppy. It also promotes a new flush of richly coloured leaves.

Miscanthus sinensis 'Hinjo'

Mixed hardy bamboos at the water's edge.

CONTAINER JUNGLE

Although this plan is for the terrace of a town house, it can easily be adapted for a balcony or even an area of a larger garden. The terrace has a small lawn beyond it, and over the garden fence there is a tall house that needs to be screened. The terrace is sunny, lying to the south of the house, but the orientation is not particularly important in this design since the effects are achieved with foliage rather than flowers. The various elements in the plan can readily be reassembled to fit or suit other situations, for example, by leaving out the large quantity of *Semiarundinaria fastuosa* if it is not needed for screening. This could well be replaced by a row of gaily coloured pelargoniums in season. It is also possible to add plants from the alternatives list (p.101) and mix them freely since both schemes are designed to achieve a generally lush, jungly feeling, evocative of holidays in hotter climates with more exotic vegetation.

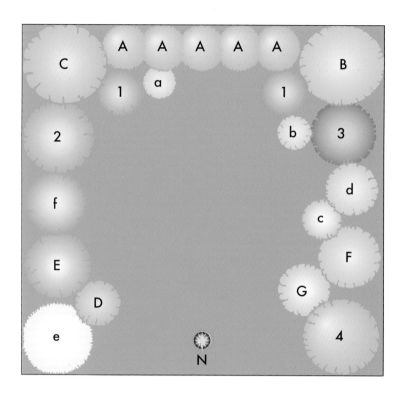

KEY

Grasses

A *Semiarundinaria fastuosa*
B *Phyllostachys nigra*
C *Miscanthus x giganteus*
D *Setaria palmifolia* or *Pleioblastus variegatus* 'Tsuboii'
E *Miscanthus sinensis* var. *condensatus* 'Cosmopolitan'
F *Miscanthus sinensis* 'Goldfeder'
G *Indocalamus hamadae*

Others

a *Aspidistra elatior* or *A. elatior* 'Variegata'
b *Cyrtomium falcatum* or *Bergenia ciliata*
c *Hosta* 'Sum and Substance'
d *Astelia chatamica*
e *Musa basjoo* or *Woodwardia unigemmata*
f *Hedychium coccineum* 'Tara'

Shrubs

1 *Cordyline australis*
2 *Butia capitata*
3 *Trachycarpus fortunei*
4 *Magnolia macrophylla*

Shrubs and grasses arranged around a small terrace.

Bamboos are ideal for creating screens. The tall, fast-growing species, *Semiarundinaria fastuosa* (A) produces a gentle barrier to disguise the neighbouring property. Like most bamboos, it does not totally obscure the house since the leaves are held high up on the canes, but it breaks up the outline and solidity of the building, which, since it is still glimpsed between the canes, is lent an air of mystery. This bamboo could equally well be planted in large pots.

Easier to manage and every bit as jungly in appearance are some of the larger grasses such as *Miscanthus x giganteus* (C), which can grow 2.5–3m (8–10ft) each season, its large, tropical-looking leaves rustling like a ballgown in the wind. Even bigger is the giant reed, *Arundo donax*, which can reach 4–5m (12–15ft) in a season. Both would make a good alternative to the phyllostachys, especially for creating a seasonal screen. In this scheme the miscanthus works as an anchor plant on one corner of the terrace. The corresponding corner to the south-west is anchored by another bamboo, *Phyllostachys nigra* (B), grown here for its striking black canes.

Watering

For pots it is worth considering installing a trickle watering system. These consist of thin, usually black, plastic hoses to which are attached at intervals small hollow spikes through which water drips. The spikes are pushed into the soil around plants in pots to keep them supplied with water. Large pots may need more than one spike. The flow of water can be controlled by a tap or valve, or by a time switch.

Several other grasses add to the jungly effect, especially *Miscanthus sinensis* var. *condensatus* 'Cosmopolitan' (E), a vigorous eulalia grass with broad leaves and dramatic white variegation, and *M. sinensis* 'Goldfeder' (F), which has narrower leaves richly variegated golden-yellow. *Setaria palmifolia* (D) is included for its vigorous growth and unusual pleated leaves, while *Indocalamus hamadae* (G) has the largest leaves of any hardy bamboo, adding a tropical quality at a lower level.

The natural companions for these bamboos and grasses are palm trees and they also intensify the jungly feel. Hardiest is the fan palm *Trachycarpus fortunei* (3), but far more tropical in appearance is *Butia capitata* (2), the hardiest of the feather palms. It is, however, rather slow to form a trunk. Providing a more instant effect is the New Zealand cabbage palm *Cordyline australis* (1), which is faster growing than either

Miscanthus sinensis 'Goldfeder'

Alternatives

The whole scene can be made richly colourful by using more plants with coloured foliage. You could even try the tender *Arundo donax* var. *versicolor*. *Musa ensete* is more colourful than *M. basjoo* (e), but also more tender. Alternatively, the dominance of greens can be relieved in summer by exotic orchids, such as cymbidiums. Cannas would add to the effect, especially the multi-coloured 'Tropicanna', also known as 'Tropical Treat', 'Durban' or 'Phasion', the white-striped 'Brunswick' and the yellow-striped 'Striatum' ('Pretoria'). And you might like to scatter small pots of *Luzula sylvatica* 'Bromel' or bright purple *Tradescantia pallida* 'Purpurea'.

This selection is suitable for a lightly shaded terrace that is sheltered from strong winds. Several of the plants are not wholly frost hardy and would need to be protected in winter. The effect is lush, colourful and nearly tropical.

Grasses

A *Hibanobambusa tranquillans* 'Shiroshima'
B *Arundo donax* var. *versicolor* tall stems and large green-and-white striped leaves
C *Pseudosasa japonica* 'Akebonosuji' cream-striped leaves
D *Stenotaphrum secundatum* 'Variegatum' trailing habit and white-striped leaves
E *Miscanthus* x *giganteus*
F *Ischyrolepis subverticillata* flamboyant restio with arching, feathery foliage
G *Pennisetum setaceum* 'Rubrum' mahogany-coloured leaves and flowers

Others

a *Fascicularia bicolor* scarlet-hearted rosettes
b *Alpinia zerumbet* 'Variegata' large green and white ginger-like leaves
c *Bilbergia nutans* bromeliad habit
d *Acanthus mollis* 'Hollard's Gold' lime-green leaves
e *Hedychium coronarium* tropical leaves and fragrant white flowers
f *Canna* 'Tropicanna' crimson-striped, dusky purple leaves
1 *Cordyline australis* 'Torbay Dazzler' multi-coloured foliage
2 *Sabal minor* huge fan-palm leaves
3 *Brahea armata* electric blue fan-palm leaves
4 *Eriobotrya japonica* large, corrugated leaves

of the others. The final structural elements of the scheme are two plants with enormous leaves, the hardy banana, *Musa basjoo* (e), and *Magnolia macrophylla* (4), whose leaves can reach nearly 1m (3ft 3in) in length when young and vigorous.

At knee level are *Aspidistra elatior* (a) with its solid, shiny leaves and the fern, *Cyrtomium falcatum* (b) – both often used as houseplants – along with the huge-leaved hosta, *H.* 'Sum and Substance' (c). *Astelia chatamica* (d) has sword-shaped silver leaves while the hardy ginger lily, *Hedychium coccineum* 'Tara' (f) is included both for its large leaves and its big, fragrant flowers.

Staking

Several of the plants in these schemes grow tall so need to be planted in wide, heavy pots to keep them stable. On balconies they may need to be tied to the railings or to the building in order to keep them upright.

Drought damage

It is essential that bamboos, especially when grown in pots, never dry out. Drought damage once done will last all season. There are trickle and drip watering systems which can help. Feed and repot container-grown bamboos every three years.

An arrangement of grasses in pots against a background of bamboo and larger grasses.

MEADOW

Wildflower meadows bring a refreshing breath of the countryside into a garden, especially to be treasured in an urban environment and, once established, they need as much or as little attention as you care to give them. In addition, they are a tempting alternative to a manicured lawn, requiring no fertilizers or pesticides, no edging or scarifying. When well done, they can be a fascinating form of 'garden', but if the soil is rich and fertile, the wild flowers will be overtaken by invasive, mat-forming grasses: on such soils prairie-style plantings are usually more successful. Meadows can be of any size, from a pocket handkerchief in a city-centre yard to several acres in the country. In a larger garden they are particularly effective when contrasted with the more formal, well-kept parts. Even in small spaces, a meadow will benefit by having a path mown through it, or mown grasses surrounding it.

Wildflower meadows do not need to be closely maintained like more formal areas.

Typical meadow wild flowers

Most will grow on most soils.
Special preferences are mentioned where relevant.

alkanet *Anchusa azurea*
bee orchid *Ophrys apifera* chalk
bloody or blood-red geranium *Geranium sanguineum* dry
buttercup *Ranunculus acris*
Cheddar pink *Dianthus gratianopolitanus*
clustered bellflower *Campanula glomerata*
columbine *Aquilegia* light soil
corn cockle *Agrostemma githago*
cornflower *Centaurea cyanus*
corn marigold *Chrysanthemum segetum*
cow parsley *Anthriscus sylvestris*
cowslip *Primula veris*
crocuses *Crocus*
dame's violet *Hesperis matronalis*
flax *Linum anglicum*
foxgloves *Digitalis purpurea* woodland margins or acid or neutral soil
Gladwyn iris, stinking iris *Iris foetidissima* dry, chalk soil
hairy violet *Viola hirta* chalk soil
lady's smock *Cardamine pratensis* damp
long smooth-headed poppy *Papaver dubium*
meadow clary, meadow sage *Salvia pratensis* well-drained
meadow cranesbill *Geranium pratense*
meadowsweet *Filipendula ulmaria* damp
melancholy thistle *Cirsium heterophyllum* damp or boggy
ox-eye daisy *Leucanthemum vulgare*
oxslip *Primula elatior*
primrose *Primula vulgaris*
purple loosestrife *Lythrum salicaria* damp
Pyrenean cranesbill *Geranium pyrenaicum* dry
red clover *Trifolium pratense*
red poppy *Papaver rhoeas* especially good on chalk
round-headed leek *Allium sphaerocephalum*
salad burnet *Sanguisorba pratensis*
selfheal *Prunella vulgaris* common in lawns
snakeshead fritillary *Fritillaria meleagris* damp, preferably alkaline
spreading bellflower *Campanula patula*
thrift *Armeria maritima* poor, sandy soil
turkscap lily *Lilium martagon* bulb
valerian *Centranthus ruber* very poor, gravelly soil

white clover *Trifolium repens*
wild carrot *Daucus carota*
wild daffodil *Narcissus pseudonarcissus*
wild honeysuckle *Lonicera periclymenum*
wild mignonette *Reseda lutea* poor, sandy soils
wood cranesbill *Geranium sylvaticum*
yarrow *Achillea millefolium*

Typical grasses

browntop *Agrostis tenuis*
common quaking grass *Briza media*
crested dog's tail grass *Cynocurus cristatus*
crested hair grass *Koeleria macrantha*
foxtail grass *Alopecurus pratensis*
meadow barley *Hordeum secalinum*
meadow fescue *Festuca pratensis*
red fescue *Festuca rubra*
sheep's fescue *Festuca ovina*
soft velvet grass *Holcus mollis*
sweet vernal grass *Anthoxanthum odoratum*
Timothy, Timothy grass *Phleum pratense*
tufted hair grass *Deschampsia cespitosa*
velvet bent grass *Agristus cannina*
yellow oat grass *Trisetum flavescens*

Soil and site preparation

The most important single consideration with a wildflower meadow is to match the plants to the soil: alkaline to alkaline, acid to acid. Also select plants suitable for sandy soil or clay, wet ground or dry, poor soil or rich. Unless you get this right, plants will not naturalize. Never dig or plough the whole area. This simply brings to the surface the multitudes of seeds which have lain dormant in the ground for perhaps a hundred years or more, and every one of them will germinate as soon as exposed to light and rain.

Meadows are by definition mown (the word comes from the Old English *mawan*), but they differ from lawns in that they are only mown once a year, preferably in autumn or winter, well after the flowering plants have shed their seeds. The reason for mowing meadows at all is to suppress the growth of woody plants such as brambles, blackthorn and hawthorns that would otherwise invade and eventually take over, ultimately turning the meadow into woodland.

Natural meadows, for example those of the English Midlands, evolve slowly over centuries and are composed of a highly complex balanced community of not only grasses and flowers but also unseen fungal mycorrhiza and micro-organisms in the soil. It is this complexity that ensures the stability of the meadow. Man-made meadows, by contrast, lack this balance and complexity and are inherently unstable – at least for the first century or so. For the first few years annuals dominate – red corn poppies (*Papaver rhoeas*) for example, followed by ox-eye daisies (*Leucanthemum vulgare*) turning the meadow first red then white – but these fade away in succeeding years as the perennials become established.

Maintenance

Mow a gently curving path through the meadow to lead the eye across it. The path will afford access allowing an intimate experience of something seemingly natural. Otherwise restrict your maintenance to being ruthless with weeding out those plants that you do not want and mowing (see box, p.106).

A beautiful flower and grass meadow in the English Midlands in early summer.

There are several different methods of making a meadow. The simplest is merely to stop mowing a lawn and see what comes up. Slightly more involved is to stop mowing and also put in native plants as 'plugs' (plants that have been raised in small pots). Further wild flowers can be added year on year to keep the meadow vibrantly colourful. Perhaps the most practical method, and often the most successful, is to weedkill the whole area, raking off the dead vegetation, and then to seed the area or plant plugs which, temporarily free from the competition of existing grasses and other vegetation, have the best chance to establish themselves before the competition re-asserts itself. The ultimate way to make a meadow with every verisimilitude of the real thing is to take a camera and go out and photograph the genuine thing in your own neighbourhood, choosing somewhere with similar soil and broad similarities of habitat to your own site, and then to recreate this meadow using the photographs to select the most suitable species and group them as they really do occur in nature. Typically, meadows are surrounded by field hedges, often a mix of colourful hawthorns, blackthorn, field maple, guelder rose and wild roses, with perhaps an occasional oak or ash growing up through the hedge. Where space permits, these elements are worth including.

Watering

English meadows evolved in an era when the annual rainfall was spread evenly across the 12 months of the year. In our times of hotter, drier summers they will need some watering to get them established.

The scheme outlined here is based on the plug-plant method, and the plants shown are those that might be added in the first year. In subsequent years, further wild flowers can be planted, particularly cow parsley in more shaded areas, snakeshead fritillaries in damper areas, wild pinks and rock roses in short meadow grass on chalky soils, and so on.

Mowing

In meadow gardening wild flowers are grown in a matrix of native grasses, so the sorts of grasses in the meadow and their control is of the first importance. Most of the taller, weedy grasses that might make a meadow look unacceptably shaggy flower late in the year and can be prevented from flowering by mowing at the right time. A suitable mowing regime is to cut three times a year, first in midsummer, when spring bulbs and early orchids are over and have seeded, the second at the very end of summer before meadow saffrons and other autumn flowers begin to bloom, and finally in late autumn before the tips of the daffodils show through the ground. Alternatively, you could mow in early summer and again in late autumn.

EARLY SUMMER BORDER

This border greets the sudden warmth of early summer with an eruption of foliage and flowers. Designed to peak early in the season, it will continue to draw the eye until late summer or even early autumn. Since most of the grasses grown in gardens flower after midsummer, it is more of a challenge to create a border specifically for early summer. The choice is more limited, though most of the grasses that do flower before midsummer are highly decorative. The scheme is designed to work in conjunction with the late summer border (pages 107–110); between them the two borders provide colour and interest from early spring to well into the winter when the grasses need to be cut down and the border tidied. Extend the season with a generous under planting of spring bulbs.

KEY

Grasses

A *Calamagrostis* x *acutiflora* 'Karl Foerster'

B *Stipa gigantea*

C *Stipa calamagrostis*

D *Deschampsia cespitosa* 'Goldtau'

E *Hordeum jubatum*

F *Pennisetum orientale* 'Robusta'

G *Stipa barbata*

H *Stipa tenuissima*

Others

a *Crambe cordifolia*

b *Selinum wallichianum*

c *Iris sibirica*

d *Baptisia australis*

e *Knautia macedonica*

f *Nepeta racemosa* 'Walker's Low'

g *Iris sibirica*

h *Astrantia* 'Hadspen Blood'

i *Hemerocallis lilioasphodelus*

j *Chaerophyllum hirsutum* 'Roseum'

k *Geranium* 'Johnson's Blue'

The border is raked from front to back, with the tallest plant, *Crambe cordifolia* (a), at the very back. This huge perennial grows clumps of rather coarse, dark green basal leaves, but in early summer it produces tall stems that branch and re-branch, each with shoots terminating in a cluster of starry white flowers; from a distance these look like great clouds of whiteness. To each side and in front of the crambe are the two most important cool-season grasses: *Stipa gigantea* (B), which throws up 2m (6ft) tall stems bearing large panicles of shimmering, gold or bronze claw-like spikelets, and *Calamagrostis* x *acutiflora* 'Karl Foerster' (A), with its stiffly upright stems topped by equally stiffly upright, narrow pinky grey panicles. Between them is a bold clump of

Stipa calamagrostis (right) and *Melica macra* (far right).

Hordeum jubatum

that most refined of cow parsleys, *Selinum wallichianum* (b) with its leaves like dark green lace and flattened heads of whitish flowers. This is flanked by the upright blue spikes of *Baptisia australis* (d) and the fragrant yellow trumpets of *Hemerocallis lilioasphodelus* (i) on the other.

The grasses at each corner of the planting mirror each other in effect, both *Deschampsia cespitosa* 'Goldtau' (D) and *Stipa tenuissima* (H) having tiny spikelets carried on the hair-like branches of much-divided panicles. Behind the deschampsia is dark crimson *Knautia macedonica* (e), and the stipa is framed by another umbellifer, *Chaerophyllum hirsutum* 'Roseum' (j), its flowers pale pink and slightly more rounded than those of the selinum. Of the front-row grasses, the beauty of *Stipa barbata* (G) is breathtaking but fleeting, its floral display lasting only a month or so, while the flowering of *Pennisetum orientale* 'Robusta' (F), once it starts, goes on until autumn, an endless succession of fluffy, pinky mauve fingers. *Hordeum jubatum* (E) is an annual that will self seed on some soils. The flowers are like long-awned barley, iridescent with a pinkish sheen, and while the main flush of flowers is produced in early

Alternatives

It is possible to produce a border with a much more cottagey look with hardy geraniums and lady's mantle spilling over the front, a traditional lupin and a cottage garden euphorbia to add structure. The colouring is altogether quieter, with the soft, pale yellows of late spring and early summer, with quiet pinks and blues enlivened by the sudden surprise of magenta. Though the scheme will need hand-weeding for its first year or two, once established the plants should be allowed to seed themselves lightly.

Grasses

A *Ampelodesmos mauritanica* arching stems and shaggy early flowers

B *Oryzopsis miliaceae* early flowering whorled panicles

C *Stipa ucrainica* needle-like spikelets

D *Carex morrowii* 'Fisher's Form' early, white and black flower spikes

E *Nassella trichotoma* haze of pink flowers early in the season

F *Melica macra* white bottlebrush flowers

G *Helictotrichon semprervirens* for its blue leaves and elegant oat-like flowers

H *Sesleria heufleriana* early flowers – with the crocuses

Others

a *Thalictrum flavum* subsp. *glaucum* tiny grey leaflets and fluffy lemon-yellow flowers

b *Salvia sclarea* var. *turkestanica* bold foliage and nacreous flowers

c *Achillea* 'Walther Funcke' flat heads of terracotta flowers

d *Geranium psilostemon* shocking magenta flowers and bold foliage

e *Geranium* 'Mrs Kendall Clark' clear blue flowers

f *Alchemilla mollis* silvery leaves and showers of acid-yellow flowers

g *Lupinus* 'Noble Maiden' spires of white flowers

h *Euphorbia characias* statuesque grey foliage and huge heads of greeny yellow flowers

i *Asphodeline lutea* slender spires of bright yellow flowers

j *Tanacetum macrophyllum* bold, flat heads of greyish white flowers

k *Stachys macrantha* vibrant magenta flowers

summer, plants will usually continue to produce a lesser succession of flowers right through the summer, often with a second good flush in late summer. *Geranium* 'Johnson's Blue' (k) is valuable for its long flowering season.

Extending the season

Crambe cordifolia looks good underplanted with *Geranium tuberosum* and all the grasses can be underplanted with bulbs, especially early, mid-season and late daffodils, tulips and camassias. In continental climates where the light is bright and clear, red and yellow tulips seem appropriate, but under the greyer skies of maritime climates, they can look garish, and quieter pinks, whites and mauves are often more harmonious.

Watering

Since this scheme will benefit from occasional watering in summer, consider laying specially designed leaky hosepipes in a serpentine fashion through the planting. Once turned on, these hoses appear to sweat water, supplying it where it is wanted – to the roots. This is particularly helpful with grasses and other tall perennials because heavy overhead watering can break stems.

Soil

The scheme is designed for reasonably average soils, neither too fertile nor too poor, neither extremely acid nor extremely alkaline. The site should, however, be well-drained; on heavy soils, such as clays, dig coarse sand or grit into the soil before you do any planting.

It pays to do any preparation of the ground several months in advance. Newly turned soil brings to the surface a multitude of weed seeds that have lain dormant, often for several decades, giving them the chance to germinate. These can be destroyed by frequent hoeing, a routine that will save weeks of hand weeding later.

Mulching

After planting it is a good idea to add a mulch to help suppress weeds. On heavy soils this should be shingle or chopped bark, but on light, quick-draining sandy soils, it is best to use a weed-suppressing fabric; hide this with a thin layer of grit or bark. Lay the fabric before planting and then make slits in it through which to plant the grasses.

Helictotrichon sempervirens with grey-leaved perennials.

LATE SUMMER BORDER

Designed as a complement to the early summer border (pages 111–114), this scheme is intended for the far left-hand corner of a garden, where the early summer border is in the right-hand corner. Together these two borders will provide colour and interest for most of the year. Late summer is the time when bedding plants and tender perennials come into their own – for those who have time to tend them. For the rest of us there are perennials and grasses that peak now and, moreover, have the bonus of going on looking good through autumn and into winter, often looking ravishing when whitened by frost. Though planned for a corner of a regularly shaped garden plot, the scheme could be adapted by straightening the corner so that it makes a single line at the back and then curving the front edge, so that the border is widest at the point opposite its tallest plants. Indeed, it could also be used in an island bed by keeping the tallest plant at the centre and wrapping the other plants all the way round it.

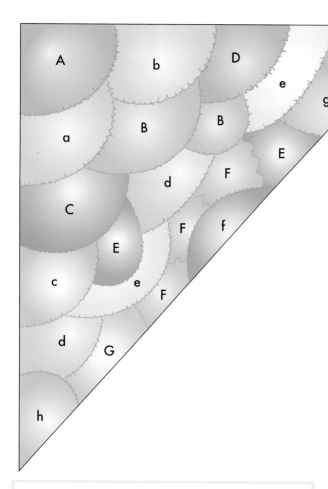

KEY

Grasses

A *Cortaderia selloana* 'Sunningdale Silver'
B *Miscanthus sinensis* 'Variegatus'
C *Panicum virgatum* 'Dallas Blues'
D *Molinia caerulea* subsp. *arundinacea* 'Bergfreund'
E *Calamagrostis brachytricha*
F *Imperata cylindrica* 'Rubra'
G *Pennisetum orientale*

Others

a *Persicaria polymorphum*
b *Eupatorium purpureum* 'Reisinschirm'
c *Verbena bonariensis*
d *Perovskia atriplicifolia* 'Blue Spire'
e *Rudbeckia fulgida* var. *sullivantii* 'Goldsturm'
f *Sedum* 'Herbstfreude' ('Autumn Joy')
g *Aster* 'Little Carlow'
h *Yucca flaccida* 'Ivory'

This border is based on the sorts of plants used by the Oehme-van Sweden partnership in their new American landscapes, which are in essence stylized prairies, stylized because they use not only genuine prairie plants but also eulalia grasses (*Miscanthus*) from China and Japan, feather reed grass (*Calamagrostis*) from Europe and stonecrops (*Sedum*) from both Europe and Asia. Such plantings are at their best after midsummer, when tall-stemmed grasses and perennials come into their own, and are most successful in continental climates with damp springs and long, dry summers. Once established they need relatively little maintenance, though hand weeding is essential until the drifts of perennials and grasses have grown together. When this has happened they will provide colour and interest from midsummer until well into the winter, and by including drifts of tulips and large-flowered alliums, the season can be started once the grasses have been cut down in late winter. The border appears to tumble down from a great height from back to front. The tallest plant is the

pampas grass, *Cortaderia selloana* 'Sunningdale Silver' (A), with its flowers towering over everything else: being both large and white, they draw the eye very strongly to them. In front of the pampas grass are two huge perennials: *Polygonum polymorphum* (a) with big, rather shaggy bunches of white flowers, and *Eupatorium purpureum* subsp. *maculatum* 'Reisinschirm' (b) with flattened heads of mauvy-purple flowers. In front and between these, striped eulalia grass (*Miscanthus sinensis* 'Variegatus'; B) ameliorates the dominance of the plumes of the pampas grass and also keeps the eye in the centre of the planting. To its left and right are two more grasses; on tall stems high above its foliage, *Molinia caerulea* subsp. *arundinacea* 'Bergfreund' (D) bears huge panicles of tiny flowers, and *Panicum virgatum* 'Dallas Blues' (C), a giant among the switch grasses, has blue leaves and large, diffuse panicles of pale flowers. The transparent quality of these flowers affords an effective contrast against the backdrop of the comparatively solid perennials.

Calamagrostis brachytricha (E) and the perennial *Perovskia atriplicifolia* 'Blue Spire' (d) are the main features in the next row towards the front of the border. Both tend to flop forward, blending their floral displays with those of the front row. They are enlivened by the upright bright yellow daisies of *Rudbeckia fulgida* var. *sullivantii* 'Goldsturm' (e).

The calamagrostis is later into flower than most grasses, and its panicles stay effective through the

Alternatives

This alternative planting scheme provides for a rather different effect, being composed of plants that do notably well in maritime climates such as that of Britain and the Pacific northwest. It is late flowering, like the main scheme, but altogether greener and leafier.

Grasses

A *Phormium tenax* 'Variegata' height and uprightness
B *Miscanthus sinensis* 'Goldfeder' rustling, gold-striped leaves
C *Panicum virgatum* 'Warrior' abundant tiny purple flowers
D *Miscanthus sinensis* 'China' flamboyant panicles
E *Molinia caerulea* subsp. *arundinacea* 'Fontäne' transparency
F *Sporobolus heterolepis* fine texture and fragrant flowers
G *Hakonechloa macra* waving green leaves

Others

a *Senecio tanguticus* cut leaves and huge heads of yellow flowers
b *Aster* 'Climax' height and showers of purplish flowers
c *Actaea cordifolia* height and curious little white flowers
d *Ceratostigma plumbaginoides* carpet of blue flowers
e *Ratibidia pinnata* height and yellow daisies
f *Sedum telephium* subsp. *maximum* 'Munstead Red' flat heads of brick-red flowers
g *Tradescantia* x *andersoniana* 'J. C. Weguelin'
h *Hemerocallis* 'Strawberry Candy'

Cortaderia selloana 'Sunningdale Silver' (far left), *Miscanthus sinensis* 'China' with agapanthus and purple beech hedging (left).

Staking

None of the plants listed needs staking. Indeed, a little laxness adds to the air of naturalness.

worst of winters, looking their best when rimed with hoar frost.

At the front of the border is a selection of plants of less than knee height, mostly with strongly coloured foliage or flowers. The richest colour of all is in the leaves of the Japanese blood grass (*Imperata cylindrica* 'Rubra'; F). They stand erect and their blood-red colouring seeps down from the tip; by late summer they are wholly red. *Aster* 'Little Carlow' (g) has rich mauvy purple daisy flowers, while *Sedum* 'Herbstfreude' (autumn joy; f) has flat heads of vivid pink. *Verbena bonariensis* (c) is a tall, slender perennial producing masses of small pink flowers at the tips of its stems. It is really only effective when planted close together in large numbers: fortunately it seeds itself freely in most soils. The yuccas are grown primarily for their foliage, but can contribute tall spikes of creamy white flowers in late summer, while *Pennisetum orientale* (G) is included because it produces its thin spikes of fluffy pink flowers from early summer until the frosts.

Maintenance

These plants should be left standing through the winter as many have interesting seedheads or skeletons. The perennials and grasses should all be cut down to 15cm (6in) from the ground in the new year, well before new growth begins in spring, and generally weeded and tidied, though any evergreens, such as pampas grasses, should be left alone.

Sedum 'Herbstfreude' (above), *Verbena bonariensis* (below left) and *Actaea cordifolia* (below right).

Appendices

This summary of information is to aid readers in the search for the most suitable grasses for their own gardens. There is a list of common names and their botanical equivalents to avoid confusion, a list of further reading as well as notable nurseries and gardens where grasses can be purchased and viewed.

Appendix I: Grasses for Special Uses

GRASSES WITH COLOURED FOLIAGE

WHITE
Pleioblastus argenteostriatus 'Akebono'

YELLOW
Carex elata 'Knightshayes'
Deschampsia flexuosa 'Tatra Gold'
Luzula sylvatica 'Aurea'
Milium effusum 'Aureum'
Pleioblastus viridistriatus
   var. chrysophyllus

BROWN
Carex buchananii
Carex comans bronze
Carex dipsacea
Carex flagellifera
Carex petriei
Carex testacea
Pennisetum macrostachyum
   'Burgundy Giant'
Pennisetum setaceum
   'Burgundy Blaze'
Pennisetum setaceum 'Rubrum'
Urcinia rubra
Urcinia uncinata (some forms)

RED
Imperata cylindrica 'Rubra'

BLACK
Ophiopogon planiscapus
   'Nigrescens'

GREY
Arundo donax
Koeleria glauca
Saccharum ravennae
Sesleria caerulea

BLUE
Alopecurus alpinus
Carex flacca
Carex flaccosperma
Carex glauca
Carex panicea
Elymus hispidus

Elymus magellanicus
Festuca glauca & cvs
Festuca valesiaca 'Silbersee'
Helictotrichon sempervirens
Koeleria glauca
Koeleria vallesiana
Leymus arenarius
Leymus racemosus
Panicum virgatum 'Blue Tower'
Panicum virgatum 'Cloud Nine'
Panicum virgatum 'Heavy Metal'
Panicum virgatum 'Pathfinder'
Panicum virgatum 'Prairie Sky'
Schizachyrium scoparium
Sorghastrum nutans 'Sentinel'
Sorghastrum nutans 'Sioux Blue'

GRASSES WITH STRIPED FOLIAGE

WHITE-STRIPED
Arrhenatherum elatius subsp. bulbosum
   'Variegatum'
Arundo donax var. versicolor
Calamagrostis x acutiflora 'Overdam'
Carex conica 'Snowline'
Carex morrowii 'Variegata'
Carex oshimensis 'Variegata'
Carex phyllocephala 'Sparkler'
Carex siderosticha 'Variegata'
Cyperus alternifolius 'Variegatus'
Dactylis glomerata 'Variegata'
Glyceria maxima var. variegata
Hibanobambusa tranquillans
   'Shiroshima'
Holcus mollis 'Albovariegatus'
Luzula sylvatica 'Marginata'
Melica uniflora 'Variegata'
Miscanthus oligostachyus 'Nanus
   Variegatus'
Miscanthus sinensis 'Dixieland'
Miscanthus sinensis 'Morning Light'
Miscanthus sinensis 'Rigoletto'
Miscanthus sinensis 'Silberpfeil'
Miscanthus sinensis 'Variegatus'
Miscanthus sinensis var. condensatus
   'Cabaret'
Miscanthus sinensis var. condensatus

'Cosmopolitan'
Molinia caerulea subsp. caerulea
   'Claerwen'
Pennisetum alopecuroides
   'Little Honey'
Phalaris arundinacea var. picta
   'Feesey'
Phalaris arundinacea var. picta 'Picta'
Phalaris arundinacea var. picta
   'Streamlined'
Pleioblastus variegatus
Sasa kurilensis 'Shima-shimofuri'
Schoenoplectus lacustris subsp.
   tabernaemontani 'Albescens'

CREAM-STRIPED
Carex morrowii 'Fisher's Form'
Carex oshimensis 'Evergold'
Glyceria maxima var. variegata
Hakonechloa macra 'Mediovariegata'
Molinia caerulea subsp. caerulea
   'Variegata'
Pleioblastus variegatus
Pleioblastus variegatus 'Tsuboii'

YELLOW-STRIPED
Alopecurus pratensis 'Aureovariegatus'
Bromus inermis 'Skinner's Gold'
Carex elata 'Aurea'
Carex oshimensis 'Evergold'
Hakonechloa macra 'Alboaurea'
Hakonechloa macra 'Aureola'
Miscanthus sinensis 'Goldfeder'
Phragmites australis 'Variegatus'
Pleioblastus viridistriatus
Pseudosasa japonica 'Akebonosuji'
Spartina pectinata 'Aureomarginata'

BANDED
Juncus effusus 'Gold Strike'
Miscanthus sinensis 'Hinjo'
Miscanthus sinensis 'Kirk Alexander'
Miscanthus sinensis 'Püenktchen'
Miscanthus sinensis 'Strictus'
Miscanthus sinensis 'Tiger Cub'
Miscanthus sinensis 'Zebrinus'
Schoenoplectus lacustris subsp.
   tabernaemontani 'Zebrinus'

AUTUMN FOLIAGE COLOUR
YELLOWS
Anemanthele lessoniana
Chasmanthium latifolium
Molinia caerulea subsp.
  arundinacea cvs
Molinia caerulea subsp. *caerulea* cvs
Panicum clandestinum
Panicum virgatum cvs
Pennisetum alopecuroides cvs
Phragmites australis

ORANGE-REDS
Andropogon gerardii
Hakonechloa macra & cvs
Miscanthus 'Purpurascens'
Saccharum ravennae
Schizachyrium scoparium
Sorghastrum nutans & cvs
Sporobolus heterolepis

BRONZE-REDS
Anemanthele arundinacea
Miscanthus sinensis 'Graziella'
Panicum virgatum 'Rotstrahlbusch'
Spodiopogon sibiricus

WINE-REDS
Hakonechloa macra & cvs
Imperata cylindrica 'Rubra'
Panicum virgatum 'Hänse Herms'
Panicum virgatum 'Shenandoah'

WOODLAND AND SHADE
Alopecurus pratensis
Alopecurus pratensis 'Aureovariegatus'
Arrhenatherum elatius subsp.
  bulbosum 'Variegatum'
Briza maxima
Briza media
Briza media 'Limouzi'
Bromus ramosus
Calamagrostis x *acutiflora* 'Karl
  Foerster'
Calamagrostis brachytricha
Carex conica 'Snowline'
Carex oshimensis 'Evergold'
Carex flaccosperma
Carex fraseri
Carex glauca
Carex 'Ice Dancer'
Carex morrowii 'Fisher's Form'

Carex morrowii 'Variegata'
Carex muskingumensis & cvs
Carex ornithopoda 'Variegata'
Carex oshimensis 'Variegata'
Carex plantaginea
Carex pendula
Carex pendula 'Moonraker'
Carex siderosticha
Carex siderosticha 'Variegata'
Carex 'Silver Sceptre'
Carex trifida
Chasmanthium latifolium
Deschampsia cespitosa & cvs
Deschampsia flexuosa & cvs
Hakonechloa macra & cvs
Holcus mollis 'Albovariegatus'
Hystrix patula
Luzula all
Melica uniflora
Melica uniflora f. *albida*
Melica uniflora 'Variegata'
Milium effusum 'Aureum
Miscanthus oligostachyus 'Afrika'
Miscanthus oligostachyus 'Herbstfeuer'
Miscanthus 'Purpurascens'
Molinia caerulea & cvs
Phalaris arundinacea & cvs
Sesleria autumnalis
Spodiopogon sibiricus
Spodiopogon sibiricus 'West Hills'

WATERSIDE GRASSES
These are grasses that need constant moisture, but will not necessarily tolerate submersion of their crowns. All the grasses listed as marginals will also grow in these conditions.

Acorus gramineus & cvs
Alopecurus pratensis
Alopecurus pratensis 'Aureovariegatus'
Arundo donax
Calamagrostis x *acutiflora* & cvs
Carex most species & cvs
Chasmanthium latifolium
Cortaderia selloana & cvs
Cyperus eragrostis
Dactylis glomerata 'Variegata'
Deschampsia cespitosa & cvs
Luzula all
Milium effusum 'Aureum'
Miscanthus sinensis & cvs

Miscanthus x *giganteus*
Molinia caerulea subsp
caerulea & cvs
Molinia caerulea subsp.
arundinacea & cvs
Panicum virgatum 'Hänse Herms'
Phalaris arundinacea & cvs
Spartina pectinata
Spartina pectinata 'Aureomarginata'

GRASSES FOR MARGINAL WATERS
These are grasses that will grow with their crowns submerged (tolerated depth shown in brackets). None has an absolute requirement for submersion, though all need constant moisture at the roots.

Acorus calamus (to 15cm/6in)
Carex glauca (to 2.5cm/1in)
Carex riparia & cvs (to 7.5cm/3in)
Cyperus longus (to 15cm/6in)
Eriophorum angustifolium
  (to 2.5cm/1in)
Eriophorum latifolium (to 10cm/4in)
Glyceria aquatica & cvs
  (to 2.5cm/1in)
Juncus effusus & cvs
  (to 10cm/4in)
Phragmites australis & cvs
  (to 60cm/2ft)
Schoenoplectus lacustris & cvs
  (to 10cm/4in)
Spartina pectinata (to 10cm/4in)
Spartina pectinata 'Aureomarginata'
  (to 10cm/4in)
Typha angustifolia (to 30cm/12in)
Typha latifolia (to 30cm/12in)
Typha minima (to 7.5cm/3in)

GRASSES FOR CLAY SOILS
Calamagrostis x *acutiflora* cvs
Deschampsia cespitosa & cvs
Phalaris arundinacea & cvs

GRASSES FOR DEEP, RICH, WELL-CULTIVATED SOILS
Miscanthus all
Saccharum ravennae

GRASSES FOR CHALK SOILS
Koeleria glauca
Melica ciliata

GRASSES REQUIRING POOR SOILS
Briza media
Bouteloua gracilis
Festuca most
Phalaris arundinacea & cvs

GRASSES REQUIRING ACID OR ALKALINE SOILS
Most grasses grow well on most soils. However, a small number have a preference for acid soils, and rather fewer a preference for alkaline. Those listed as needing acid soils will grow well in soils that range from neutral (pH 7) to severely acid (pH 3.5), but will not flourish in soils on the alkaline side of neutral. Similarly, those listed as needing alkaline soils will grow in soils that range from neutral (pH 7) to severely alkaline (pH 8.5) but will not flourish in soils on the acid side of neutral. There are a few exceptions: *Bouteloua gracilis*, *Cynodon dactylis* and *Phleum pratense* will thrive on acid, alkaline or neutral soils.

FOR ACID SOILS
Arrhenatherum elatius subsp. *bulbosum*
Arrhenatherum elatius subsp. *bulbosum* 'Variegatum'
Bouteloua gracilis
Briza maxima
Deschampsia flexuosa
Holcus mollis 'Albovariegatus'
Molinia caerulea & forms & cvs
Pennisetum alopecuroides & cvs
Phalaris arundinacea & cvs

FOR ALKALINE SOILS
Andropogon gerardii
Bouteloua gracilis
Koeleria cristata
Milium effusum 'Aureum'

GRASSES FOR SANDY SOILS
Spartina pectinata 'Aureomarginata'

GRASSES FOR SHADE
Alopecurus pratensis 'Aureovariegatus'
Arrhenatherum elatius subsp. *bulbosum* 'Variegatum'
Briza media
Calamagrostis x *acutiflora* 'Karl Foerster'
Calamagrostis brachytricha
Carex fraseri
Chasmanthium latifolium
Deschampsia caespitosa & cvs
Deschampsia flexuosa & cvs
Hakonechloa macra & cvs
Hystrix patula
Luzula all
Melica ciliata
Melica uniflora
Milium effusum 'Aureum'
Miscanthus 'Purpurascens'
Molinia caerulea & cvs
Phalaris arundinacea & cvs
Sesleria autumnalis
Sesleria heufleriana
Spodiopogon sibiricus

DROUGHT-TOLERANT GRASSES
Andropogon gerardii
Bouteloua gracilis
Eragrostis chloromelas
Eragrostis curvula
Festuca glauca
Festuca valesiaca
Helictotrichon sempervirens
Holcus mollis 'Albovariegatus'
Koeleria glauca
Koeleria vallesiana
Leymus arenarius
Melica altissima
Oryzopsis miliacea
Panicum virgatum & cvs
Pennisetum all
Sesleria autumnalis
Schizachyrium scoparium
Sorghastrum nutans & cvs
Sporobolus airoides
Stipa barbata
Stipa calamagrostis
Stipa capillata
Stipa gigantea
Stipa pennata
Stipa tenuissima

ANNUAL GRASSES
Agrostis nebulosa
Aira elegantissima
Avena sterilis
Briza maxima
Briza minor
Briza madritensis
Lagurus ovatus
Lamarckia aurea
Panicum miliaceum 'Violaceum'
Pennisetum setaceum
Phalaris canariensis
Polypogon monspeliensis
Setaria glauca
Sorghum bicolor
Zea mays

GRASSES FOR TUSSOCK GARDENS
Carex albula
Carex buchananii
Carex comans
Carex comans bronze
Carex comans 'Frosted Curls'
Carex dipsacea
Carex flagellifera
Carex petriei
Carex tenuiculmis
Carex testacea
Carex trifida
Chionochloa conspicua
Chionochloa flavescens
Chionochloa flavicans
Chionochloa rubra
Cortaderia fulvida
Cortaderia richardii
Uncinia rubra

GRASSES FOR POTS, TUBS AND CONTAINERS OUTSIDE
Anemanthele arundinacea
Carex albula
Carex buchananii
Carex comans

Carex comans 'Frosted Curls'
Carex dolichostachya 'Kaga-Nishiki'
Carex elata 'Aurea'
Carex oshimensis 'Variegata'
Carex petriei
Carex 'Taranaki'
Chasmanthium latifolium
Cortaderia selloana 'Pumila'
Elymus magellanicus
Elymus hispidus
Festuca glauca & cvs
Glyceria maxima
Glyceria maxima var. variegata
Hakonechloa macra & cvs
Helictotrichon sempervirens
Holcus mollis 'Albovariegatus'
Imperata cylindrica 'Rubra'
Leymus arenarius
Luzula sylvatica & cvs
Milium effusum 'Aureum'
Miscanthus 'Purpurascens'
Miscanthus sinensis most cvs
Molinia caerulea & cvs
Phalaris arundinacea & cvs
Pennisetum alopecuroides & cvs
Pennisetum setaceum
    'Burgundy Blaze'
Pennisetum villosum
Pleioblastus variegatus
Pleioblastus viridistriatus
Stipa tenuissima
Uncinia rubra

GRASSES FOR ALPINE GARDENS
Agrostis canina 'Silver Needles'
Alopecurus alpinus
Bouteloua gracilis
Carex conica 'Snowline'
Festuca gautieri 'Pic Carlit'
Festuca eskia
Holcus mollis 'Variegatus'
Melica ciliata

GRASSES FOR MIXED BORDERS
Achnatherum calamagrostis
Ampelodesmos mauritanica
Andropogon all
Arundo donax

Bouteloua gracilis
Bromus most
Briza maxima
Briza media
Briza media 'Limouzi'
Calamagrostis x acutiflora & cvs
Calamagrostis brachytricha
Carex pendula
Carex pendula 'Moonraker'
Chasmanthium latifolium
Cortaderia fulvida
Cortaderia richardii
Cortaderia selloana & cvs
Deschampsia cespitosa & cvs
Deschampsia flexuosa & cvs
Elymus hispidus
Eragrostis chloromelas
Eragrostis curvula
Festuca cushion-forming species
Helictotrichon sempervirens
Hordeum jubatum
Hystrix patula
Lagurus ovatus
Lagurus ovatus 'Nanus'
Leymus arenarius
Luzula nivea
Melica altissima 'Alba'
Melica altissima 'Atropurpurea'
Melica ciliata
Melica transsilvanica
Milium effusum & cvs
Miscanthus x giganteus
Miscanthus sinensis & cvs
Molinia most
Panicum virgatum & cvs
Pennisetum alopecuroides & cvs
Pennisetum macrourum
Pennisetum orientale
Pennisetum villosum
Schizachyrium scoparium
Sorghastrum nutans & cvs
Spartina pectinata 'Aureomarginata'
Spodiopogon sibiricus
Stipa gigantea
Stipa tenuissima
And most annual grasses

GRASSES FOR MEADOWS
Agrostis canina
Alopecurus pratensis
Briza media

Deschampsia cespitosa
Festuca rubra
Holcus mollis

GRASSES FOR WILDFLOWER LAWNS
Deschampsia flexuosa
Festuca rubra
Holcus mollis

ORNAMENTAL BRITISH NATIVE SPECIES
Agrostis canina
Apera spica-venti
Briza media
Bromus several
Carex flacca
Carex panicea
Carex pendula
Carex riparia
Cyperus longus
Deschampsia cespitosa
Deschampsia flexuosa
Eriophorum
Glyceria maxima
Juncus all
Koeleria cristata
Lagurus ovatus
Leymus arenarius
Luzula sylvatica
Molinia caerulea
Phleum pratense
Schoenoplectus
Stipa pennata

GRASSES THAT TOLERATE SALT WIND AND SALT SPRAY
Ampelodesmos mauritanica
Bromus inermis
Carex testacea
Chasmanthium latifolium
Cortaderia fulvida
Cortaderia richardii
Cortaderia selloana
Leymus arenarius
Panicum virgatum
Phalaris arundinacea & cvs
Phragmites australis & cvs
Spartina pectinata

EVERGREEN GRASSES

Ampelodesmos mauritanica
Bamboos all
Carex albula
Carex buchananii
Carex comans
Carex conica 'Snowline'
Carex dipsacea
Carex flagellifera
Carex fraseri
Carex oshimensis & cvs
Carex morrowii & cvs
Carex pendula
Carex petriei
Carex testacea
Carex trifida
Chionochloa rubra
Cortaderia all
Deschampsia cespitosa & cvs
Juncus all
Koeleria all
Luzula all
Sesleria all
Stipa gigantea
Uncinia all

DROUGHT-TOLERANT GRASSES

Andropogon gerardii
Anemanthele arundinacea
Calamagrostis × *acutiflora*
Calamagrostis brachytricha
Carex buchananii
Carex conica 'Snowline'
Carex dipsacea
Carex dolichostachya 'Kaga-Nishiki'
Carex flaccosperma
Carex flagellifera
Carex glauca
Carex morrowii & cvs
Carex oshimensis & cvs
Carex petriei
Carex comans 'Taranaki'
Carex testacea
Deschampsia cespitosa all
Luzula sylvatica all
Molinia caerulea all
Miscanthus all
Panicum virgatum all
Pennisetum alopecuroides & cvs
Phalaris arundinacea & cvs

Phyllostachys aureosulcata var. spectabilis
Phyllostachys bambusoides 'Holochrysa'
Phyllostachys bambusoides 'Castillonis'
Phyllostachys nigra
Phyllostachys vivax 'Aureocaulis'
Pleioblastus variegatus
Pleioblastus variegatus 'Tsuboii'
Pleioblastus viridistriatus
Pseudosasa japonica 'Akebonosuji'
Sasa kurilensis 'Shimofuri'
Schizachyrium scoparium
Sorghastrum nutans & cvs
Spartina pectinata 'Aureomarginata'
Spodiopogon sibiricus
Stipa tenuissima
Typha most
Uncinia rubra

GRASSES FOR CUTTING

D = good for drying
S = may shatter if not picked early enough
Ss = inclined to shatter even when picked early, and not to be relied upon in permanent arrangements

Agrostis D
Aira elegantissima D
Ampelodesmos mauritanica D
Arundo donax D
Avena
Bouteloua gracilis D
Briza all D
Bromus most D
Calamagrostis all
Chasmanthium latifolium D
Cortaderia all D
Deschampsia cespitosa & cvs
Deschampsia flexuosa & cvs
Elymus most
Eragrostis all
Hordeum jubatum Ss
Hystrix patula S
Lagurus ovatus D
Lamarckia aurea Ss
Leymus
Luzula
Melica altissima & cvs
Milium effusum

Miscanthus all D
Panicum all
Pennisetum all S
Phalaris canariensis D
Phragmites australis D
Saccharum ravennae D
Schizachyrium scoparium D
Setaria italica
Sorghastrum nutans & cvs D
Sorghum all D
Spartina pectinata
Stipa calamagrostis
Stipa capillata
Typha all D
Uniola latifolia
Zea mays D

GRASSES FOR HOUSE, GREENHOUSE AND CONSERVATORY

Arundo donax var. *versicolor*
Carex muskingumensis 'Oehme'
Carex oshimensis & cvs
Carex phyllocephala 'Sparkler'
Cyperus alternifolius
Cyperus alternifolius 'Variegata'
Cyperus papyrus
Hibanobambusa tranquillans 'Shiroshima'
Phyllostachys aurea 'Holochrysa'
Phyllostachys bambusoides 'Castillonis'
Phyllostachys bambusoides 'Castillonis Inversa'
Phyllostachys bambusoides 'Holochrysa'
Phyllostachys nigra
Phyllostachys nigra 'Boryana'
Pleioblastus argenteostriatus 'Akebono'
Pleioblastus variegatus
Pleioblastus variegatus 'Tsuboii'
Pseudosasa japonica 'Akebonosuji'
Sasa kurilensis 'Shimofuri'

GRASSES FOR FRAGRANCE

Anthoxanthum odoratum
Sporobolus heterolepis

AWARD OF GARDEN MERIT GRASSES AND GRASS-LIKE PLANTS

The Award of Garden Merit, as reinstated in 1992 recognizes plants of outstanding excellence for garden decoration or use, whether grown in the open or under glass.

Aira elegantissima
Carex buchananii
Carex elata 'Aurea', *C. e.* Knightshayes'
Carex oshimensis 'Evergold'
Chusquea culeou
Cortaderia richardii
Cortaderia selloana 'Aureolineata',
  C. s. 'Pumila', *C. s.* 'Sunningdale Silver'

Cyperus papyrus
Fargesia murielae, F. m. 'Simba'
Fargesia nitida 'Nymphenburg'
Festuca glauca 'Blaufuchs'
Hakonechloa macra 'Alboaurea'
H. m. 'Aureola'
Helictotrichon sempervirens
Hibanobambusa tranquillans
  'Shiroshima'
Indocalamus tessellatus
Lagurus ovatus
Milium effusum 'Aureum'
Miscanthus sinensis 'Flamingo',
  'Gewitterwolke', 'Ghana', 'Gold und
  Silber', 'Grosse Fontäne', 'Kaskade',
  'Kleine Fontäne', 'Kleine Silberspinne',
  'Morning Light', 'Septemberrot',
  'Silberfeder', 'Silberspinne', 'Strictus',
  'Undine', 'Variegatus', 'Zebrinus'

M. s. var. *condensatus* 'Cosmopolitan'
Molinia caerulea subsp. *caerulea*
  'Variegata'
Ophiopogon planiscapus 'Nigrescens'
Pennisetum orientale
Pennisetum setaceum
Pennisetum villosum
Phalaris arundinacea var. *picta* 'Picta'
Phyllostachys aurea
Phyllostachys aureosulcata
  f. *aureocaulis, P. a.* f. *spectabilis*
Phyllostachys nigra
Phyllostachys nigra f. *henonis*
Phyllostachys vivax f. *aureocaulis*
Pleioblastus variegatus
Pleioblastus viridistriatus
Pseudosasa japonica
Semiarundinaria fastuosa
Stipa gigantea

Appendix II: Further Reading

Chao, C.S., *A Guide to Bamboos Grown in Britain*, The Royal Botanic Gardens, Kew, London, 1989.
Chapman, G.P., & Peat, W.E., *An Introduction to the Grasses*, C.A.B. International, Oxford, 1992.
Darke, F.P., *Ornamental Grasses at Longwood Gardens*, Longwood Gardens Inc., Kennet Square, Pennsylvania, 1990.
Darke, Rick, *Ornamental Grasses for your Garden*, Michael Friedman Publishing Group, London & New York, 1994.
Fitter, R., Fitter, A., & Farrer, A., *Collins Pocket Guide to Grasses, Sedges, Rushes & Ferns*, Harper Collins, 1984.
Greenlee, John, *The Encyclopedia of Ornamental Grasses*, Rodale Press, Pennsylvania, 1992.
Griffiths, Professor D.A., *Grasses & Sedges of Hong Kong*, The Urban Council of Hong Kong, 1983.
Hansen, Richard, & Sachs, Friedrich, *Perennials and their Garden Habitats*, Cambridge University Press, Cambridge, 1993.
Kingsbury, Noel, *The New Perennial Garden*, Frances Lincoln, London, 1996.
Loewer, Peter, *Ornamental Grasses*, Brooklyn Botanic Garden, New York, 1988.
Loewer, Peter, *Ornamental Grasses*, Better Homes and Gardens Books, Des Moines, 1995.
Oakes, A. J., *Ornamental Grasses and Grasslike Plants*, Van Nostrand Reinhold, New York, 1990.
Oehme, Wolfgang and van Sweden, James, *Bold Romantic Gardens*, Acropolis Books Ltd, Reston, Virginia, 1990.
Ottesen, Carole, *Ornamental Grasses, The Amber Wave*, McGraw-Hill, New York, 1989.
Philips, Roger & Rix, Martin, *Perennials*, Pan Books Ltd, London, 1991.
Recht, Christine, & Wetterwald, Max F., *Bamboos*, Timber Press, Portland, Oregon, 1992.
Reinhardt, Thomas A., Reinhardt, Martina, and Moskowitz, Mark, *Ornamental Grass Gardening*, Macdonald Orbis, New York, 1989.
Romanowski, Nick, *Grasses, Bamboos and Related Plants in Australia*, Thomas C. Lothian Pty Ltd, Melbourne, 1993.
Rose, Francis, *Grasses, Sedges, Rushes and Ferns of the British Isles and North-western Europe*, Viking, London, 1989.
Royal Horticultural Society, The, *Award of Garden Merit Plants*, The Royal Horticultural Society, London, 1993.
Ryves, T.B., Clement, E.J. & Foster, M.C., *Alien Grasses of the British Isles*, Botanical Society of the British Isles, London, 1996.
Speichert, Greg, *Miscanthus Checklist*, Crystal Palace Perennials, St John, Illinois, 1994.
Taylor, Nigel J., *Ornamental Grasses, Bamboos, Rushes and Sedges*, Ward Lock, London, 1992.
Walters, S. M. et al, *The European Garden Flora, Vol II*, Cambridge University Press, Cambridge, 1984.

Appendix III: List of Common Names

African love grass *Eragrostis curvula*
alkali dropseed *Sporobolus airoides*
alpine fox-tail grass *Alopecurus alpinus*
American galingale *Cyperus eragrostis*
animated oat *Avena sterilis*
annual beard grass *Polypogon monspeliensis*
annual setaria *Setaria italica* 'Macrochaeta'
Argentinian pampas grass *Cortaderia selloana*
autumn moor grass *Sesleria autumnalis*
beard grass *Andropogon* species, *Polypogon monspeliensis*
bearskin fescue *Festuca gautieri*
Bend love grass *Eragrostis trichodes* 'Bend'
big bluestem *Andropogon gerardii*
birdseed grass *Phalaris canariensis*
bird's foot sedge *Carex ornithopoda*
black bamboo *Phyllostachys nigra*
black-flowered sedge *Carex nigra*
black millet *Sorghum nigrum*
blonde sedge *Carex comans*
blood grass *Imperata cylindrica* 'Rubra'
blue fescue *Festuca glauca*
blue grama *Bouteloua gracilis*
blue-green hair grass *Sesleria heufleriana*
blue hair grass *Koeleria glauca*
blue Indian grass *Sorghastrum nutans* 'Sioux Blue'
blue lyme grass *Leymus arenarius*
blue moor grass *Sesleria caerulea*
blue oat grass *Helictotrichon sempervirens*
blue wheatgrass *Elymus hispidus*
Boer love grass *Eragrostis chloromelas*
bottle-brush grass *Hystrix patula*
Bowles' golden grass *Milium effusum* 'Aureum'
Bowles' golden sedge *Carex elata* 'Aurea'
broad-leaved cotton grass *Eriophorum latifolium*
broad-leaved sedge *Carex plantaginea*
broad-leaved snow grass *Chionochloa flavescens*
broad-leaved snow tussock *Chionochloa flavescens*
brome *Bromus* species
brome grass *Bromus* species
broom sedge *Andropogon virginicus*
brown bent *Agrostis canina*

Buchanan's brown sedge *Carex buchananii*
bulbous couch grass *Arrhenatherum elatius*
bulbous oat grass *Arrhenatherum elatius* subsp. *bulbosum*
bulrush *Schoenoplectus lacustris*, *Typha* species
bushy beard grass *Andropogon glomeratus*
Canary grass *Phalaris arundinacea*
carnation grass *Carex flacca*, *Carex panicea*
carnation sedge *Carex flacca*, *Carex panicea*
cat-tails *Typha* species
Chinese mountain bamboo *Fargesia* species
Christ's tears *Coix lachryma-jobi*
cloud grass *Agrostis nebulosa*
clubrushes *Schoenoplectus*
cocksfoot grass *Dactylis glomerata*
common bulrush *Typha minima*
common cat-tail *Typha minima*
common cotton grass *Eriophorum angustifolium*
common quaking grass *Briza media*
common reed *Phragmites australis*
common soft rush *Juncus effusus*
compact brome *Bromus madritensis*
corkscrew Baltic rush *Juncus balticus* 'Spiralis'
corkscrew rush *Juncus effusus* 'Spiralis'
corn *Zea mays*
cotton grass *Eriophorum* species
creeping red fescue *Festuca rubra*
creeping soft grass *Holcus mollis*
crested hair grass *Koeleria macrantha*
crimson fountain grass *Pennisteum setaceum* 'Rubrum'
deer-tongue grass *Panicum clandestinum*
didder *Briza media*
dickies *Briza media*
doddering dillies *Briza media*
dropseed *Sporobolus* species
dwarf cat-tail *Typha minima*
Egyptian paper reed *Cyperus papyrus*
esparto grass *Stipa tenacissima*
Ethiopian fountain grass *Pennisetum villosum*
eulalia grass *Miscanthus sinensis*
European feather grass *Stipa tenuissima*
fairy grass *Deschampsia flexuosa*

feather grass *Stipa pennata*
feather grasses *Stipa* species
feather reed grass *Calamagrostis* x *acutiflora*
fescue *Festuca* species
flame grass *Miscanthus oligostachyus* 'Purpurascens'
forest blue grass *Poa chaixii*
fountain grass *Pennisetum alopecuroides*
fountain sedge *Carex dolichostachya*
fox-tail bamboo *Chusquea couleou*
fox-tail grass *Alopecurus pratensis*
fox-tail millet *Setaria italica* 'Macrochaeta'
Fraser's sedge *Carex fraseri*
galingale *Cyperus longus*
giant fescue *Festuca gigantea*
giant reed *Arundo donax*
golden bamboo *Phyllostachys aurea*
golden fox-tail grass *Alopecurus pratensis* 'Aureovariegata'
golden Hakone grass *Hakonechloa macra* 'Alboaurea' or 'Aureola'
golden oat grass *Stipa gigantea*
golden oats *Stipa gigantea*
golden toupee fescue *Festuca glauca* 'Golden Toupee'
goldentop *Lamarckia aurea*
gossamer grass *Anemanthele lessoniana*
great millet *Sorghum nigrum*, *Sorghum bicolor*
great weeping sedge *Carex pendula*
greater pond sedge *Carex riparia*
greater quaking grass *Briza maxima*
greater woodrush *Luzula sylvatica*
hair grass *Deschampsia cespitosa*, *Aira elegantissima*
Hakone grass *Hakonechloa macra*
hairy brome *Bromus ramosus*
hard rush *Juncus inflexus*
hare's tail *Lagurus ovatus*
hook sedges *Uncinia* species
hog millet *Panicum miliaceum*
Hunangamoho grass *Chionochloa conspicua*
Indian corn *Zea mays*
Indian grass *Sorghastrum nutans*
inflexible rush *Juncus effusus*
Japanese blood grass *Imperata cylindrica* 'Rubra'
Japanese silver grass *Miscanthus sinensis* var. *condensatus*
Job's tears *Coix lachryma-jobi*

Kakaho *Cortaderia fulvida*
Korean feather reed grass *Stipa brachytricha*
large quaking grass *Briza maxima*
lesser quaking grass *Briza media*
lesser reed mace *Typha minima*
little bluestem *Schizachyrium scoparium*
love grass *Eragrostis* species
loose silky bent *Apera spica-venti*
maiden grass *Miscanthus sinensis* 'Gracillimus'
maize *Zea mays*
mana grass *Glyceria maxima*
Mauritanian rope grass *Ampelodesmos mauritanicus*
Mauritanian vine reed *Ampelodesmos mauritanicus*
meadow barley *Hordeum secalinum*
meadow fountain grass *Pennisetum incomptum*
meadow fox-tail grass *Alopecurus pratensis*
melic *Melica* species
Mexican feather grass *Stipa tenuissima*
millet *Milium* species, *Sorghum* species
moor grass *Molinia* species, *Sesleria* species
Morrow's sedge *Carex morrowii*
mosquito grass *Bouteloua gracilis*
needle grass *Stipa* species, *Achnatherum calamagrostis*
New Zealand blue meadow grass *Poa colensoi*
New Zealand blue sedge *Carex trifida* var. *chatamica*
New Zealand everbrown sedge *Carex buchananii*
New Zealand feather grass *Stipa arundinacea*
New Zealand hair sedge *Carex comans*
New Zealand pampas grass *Cortaderia richardii*
New Zealand tussock *Chionochloa* species
nodding melic *Melica nutans*
North American blue sedge *Carex glauca*
northern sea oats *Chasmanthium latifolium*
orange sedge *Carex testacea*
orange New Zealand sedge *Carex testacea*
orchard grass *Dactylis glomerata*
oriental fountain grass *Pennisetum orientale*
pale galingale *Cyperus eragrostis*
palm grass *Setaria palmifolia*

palm-leaf sedge *Carex muskingumensis*
pampas grass *Cortaderia selloana*
panic grass *Panicum virgatum*
papyrus *Cyperus papyrus*
pendulous sedge *Carex pendula*
perennial quaking grass *Briza media*
Petriei's brown sedge *Carex petriei*
pheasant grass *Anemanthele lessoniana*
plantain sedge *Carex plantaginea*
plantain-leaved sedge *Carex plantaginea*
plumed tussock grass *Chionochloa conspicua*
pony-tail grass *Stipa tenuissima*
prairie cord grass *Spartina pectinata*
prairie dropseed *Sporobolus heterolepis*
Provençal reed *Arundo donax*
purple hog millet *Panicum miliaceum* 'Violaceum'
purple love grass *Eragrostis spectabilis*
purple millet *Panicum miliaceum* 'Violaceum'
purple moor grass *Molinia caerulea* subsp. *caerulea*
quaking grass *Briza* species
rabbit's foot grass *Polypogon monspeliensis*
rabbit-tail grass *Lagurus ovatus*
Ravenna grass *Saccharum ravennae*
red fescue *Festuca rubra*
red New Zealand hook sedge *Uncinia rubra*
red-seeded switch grass *Panicum virgatum* 'Rubrum'
red snow grass *Chionochloa rubra*
red tussock grass *Chionochloa rubra*
reed *Phragmites australis*
reed canary grass *Phalaris arundinacea*
reed grass *Calamagrostis* species
reeds *Juncus* species
ribbon grass *Phalaris arundinacea*
rice grass *Oryzopsis* species
riparian sedge *Carex riparia*
rope grass *Ampelodesmos mauritanicus*
rush *Juncus* species
sand love grass *Eragrostis trichodes*
Siberian melic *Melica altissima*
side-oats grama *Bouteloua curtipendula*
silky-spike melic *Melica ciliata*
silver spear grass *Achnatherum calamagrostis*
smilo grass *Oryzopsis miliacea*
smooth brome *Bromus inermis*
snow grasses *Chionochloa* species
snow tussock *Chionochloa rigida*
snowy woodrush *Luzula nivea*
soft rush *Juncus effusus*

soft velvet grass *Holcus mollis*
Spanish oat grass *Stipa gigantea*
spring moor grass *Sesleria heuffleriana*
squirrel tail barley *Hordeum jubatum*
striped cocksfoot grass *Dactylis glomerata* 'Variegata'
striped feather reed grass *Calamagrostis* × *acutiflora* 'Overdam'
striped prairie cord grass *Spartina pectinata* 'Aureomarginata'
sugar cane *Saccharum officinarum*
sweet corn *Zea mays*
sweet flag *Acorus calamus*
sweet reed grass *Glyceria maxima*
sweet galingale *Cyperus longus*
sweet manna grass *Glyceria* species
switch grass *Panicum virgatum*
tall moor grass *Molinia caerulea* subsp. *arundinacea*
toe-toe *Cortaderia fulvida*, *Cortaderia richardii*
trip-me-up *Carex testacea*
true millet *Sorghum bicolor*
tufted hair grass *Deschampsia cespitosa*
tumble grass *Eragrostis spectabilis*
turkey foot *Andropogon gerardii*
umbrella plant *Cyperus alternifolius*
umbrella plants *Cyperus* species
umbrella sedges *Cyperus* species
vanilla grass *Hierochloë odorata*
velvet bent grass *Agrostis canina*
wavy hair grass *Deschampsia flexuosa*
weeping love grass *Eragrostis curvula*
weeping sedge *Carex pendula*
wheatgrass *Elymus* species
white-top sedge *Rhynchorspora* species
wild oat *Avena sterilis*
wild oats *Chasmanthium latifolium*
wild rice *Zizania aquatica*
wild rye *Elymus* species
wind grass *Anemanthele lessoniana*
wood blue grass *Poa chaixii*
wood brome *Bromus ramosus*
wood melic *Melica uniflora*
wood millet *Milium effusum*
wood oats *Chasmanthium latifolium*
woodrush *Luzula sylvatica*
wood sedge *Carex sylvatica*
Yorkshire fog *Holcus lanatus*
zebra grass *Miscanthus sinensis* 'Zebrinus'

Appendix IV:
Where to See Ornamental Grasses

UK

Blooms of Bressingham
Bressingham, Diss
Norfolk IP22 2AB
www.bloomsofbressingham.co.uk

Bury Court
Bentley, Farnham
Surrey GU10 5LZ
(National Garden Scheme Days only)

Hall Farm Nursery
Vicarage Lane
Kinnerley
Nr. Oswestry
Shropshire SY10 8DH

Hoecroft Plants
Severals Grange
Holt Road
Wood Norton
Dereham
Norfolk NR20 5BL
www.hoecroft.co.uk

Jungle Giants
Burford House Gardens
Tenbury Wells
Worcestershire WR15 8HQ
www.junglegiants.co.uk

Mozart House Nursery
Garden
84 Central Avenue
Wigston Magna
Wigston
Leicesteshire LE18 2AA
By appointment only.
Tel. 0116 288 9548

The Beth Chatto Garden Ltd
Elmstead Market
Colchester
Essex CO7 7DB
info@bethchatto.fsnet.co.uk

The Campbell-Sharp Grassery
Marlborough, Wiltshire
Strictly by appointment only.
Tel. 01672 515380

The Knoll Garden
Hampreston, Stapehill
Nr. Wimborne
Dorset BH21 7ND
www.knollgardens.co.uk

Royal Botanic Gardens
Kew
Richmond
Surrey TW9 3AE.

Royal Horticultural Society Garden
Rosemoor
Great Torrington
North Devon EX38 8PH

The Royal Horticultural Society
Garden
Wisley, Woking
Surrey GU23 6QB

CANADA

Free Spirit Nursery
20405 – 32 Avenue
Langley, BC V2Z 2C7

EUROPE

Karl-Foerster Garten
Amundsenstrasse
Potsdam
Germany

Le Jardin Plume
Le Thil
76116 Auzouville sur Ry
France
lejardinplume@fnac.net

Piet Oudolf
Broekstraat 17
6999 de Hummelo
Holland
www.oudolf.com

USA

Greenlee Nursery
301 Franklin Avenue
Pomona, CA 91766

Kurt Bluemel Inc.
2740 Greene Lane
Baldwin, MD 21013
www.kurtbluemel.com

Longwood Gardens
US Route 1
Kennett Square
PA 19348
www.longwoodgardens.org

Manito Park
Spokane,
Washington

Plant Delights Nursery Inc.
Juniper Level Botanic Gardens
9241 Sauls Road
Raleigh, NC 27603
www.plantdelights.com

The Donald M. Kendall
Sculpture Garden
PepsiCo Headquarters
Purchase, New York
(Features a grass garden designed by
Russell Page)

Where to buy Ornamental Grasses

UK

Drysdale Garden Exotics
Bowerwood Road
Fordingbridge
Hampshire SP6 1BN

Hall Farm Nursery
Vicarage Lane
Kinnerley
Nr. Oswestry
Shropshire SY10 8DH
www.hallfarmnursery.co.uk

Hoecroft Plants
Severals Grange
Holt Road
Wood Norton
Dereham
Norfolk NR20 5BL
www.hoecroft.co.uk

John Chambers Wild
Flower Seeds
15 Westleigh Road
Barton Seagrave
Kettering
Northamptonshire
NN15 5AJ.

The Knoll Garden
Hampreston
Stapehill
Nr. Wimborne
Dorset BH21 7ND
www.knollgardens.co.uk

Marchants Hardy Plants
2 Marchants Cottages
Ripe Road
Laughton
East Sussex BN8 6AJ

Monksilver Nursery
Oakington Road
Cottenham
Cambridge CB4 8TW
www.monksilver.com

Mozart House Nursery
Garden
84 Central Avenue, Wigston
Leicestershire LE18 2AA.
By appointment only.
Tel: 0116 288 9548

Pennard Plants
The Walled Gardens,
East Pennard
Shepton Mallet
Somerset BA4 6TP
www.pennardplants.com

Phoenix Plants
Paice Lane
Medstead, Alton
Hampshire GU34 5PR
greenfarmplants.Marina.Chri
stopher@Care4free.net

The Big Grass Company
Hookhill Plantation
Woolfardisworthy East
Black Dog, Nr. Crediton
Devon EX17 4RH
www.big-grass-co.co.uk

The Beth Chatto
Gardens Ltd.
Elmstead Market
Colchester
Essex CO7 7DB
info@bethchatto.fsnet.co.uk

The Ornamental Grass
Nursery
Church Farm
Westgate
Rillington, Malton
North Yorkshire YO17 8LN
www.ornamentalgrass.co.uk

The Plantsman's Preference
Lynwood, Hopton Road
Garboldisham, Diss
Norfolk IP 22 2QN
www.plantpref.co.uk

CANADA

Blue Stem Nursery
1946 Fife Road
Christina Lake
BC, V0H 1E3
mneale@bluestem.ca

EUROPE

Bambous de Planbuisson
Rue Montaigne
24480 Le Buisson-de-
Cadouin
France
www.planbuisson.com

Crea'Paysage
Lannenec
56270 Ploemeur
France
creapaysage@wanadoo.fr

Didier Marchand
La Cordonnaie
35560 Bazouges La Perouse
France

Le Jardin Plume
Le Thil
76116 Auzouville sur Ry
France
lejardinplume@fnac.net

Piet Oudolf
Broekstraat 17
6999 de Hummelo
Holland.
www.oudolf.com

USA

Andre Viette Farm & Nursery
Route 1, Box 16
Fishersville, VA 22939

Carroll Gardens
444 East Main Street
P.O. Box 310
Westminster, MD 21157
www.carrollgardens.com

Greenlee Nursery
301 E. Franklin Avenue
Pomona, CA 91766

Kurt Bluemel Inc.
2740 Greene Lane
Baldwin MD 21013
www.kurtbluemel.com

Limerock Ornamental
Grasses
R.D. 1, Box 111-C
Port Matilda, PA 16870
www.limerockgrasses.com

New England Bamboo
Company
5 Granite Street
Rockport, MA 01966
www.newengbamboo.com

Plant Delights Nursery Inc.
Juniper Levels Botanic
Gardens
9241 Sauls Road
Raleigh NC 27603
www.plantdelights.com

Wayside Gardens
1 Garden Lane, Hodges
SC 29696-0001
www.waysidegardens.com

Plant Hardiness Zone Map

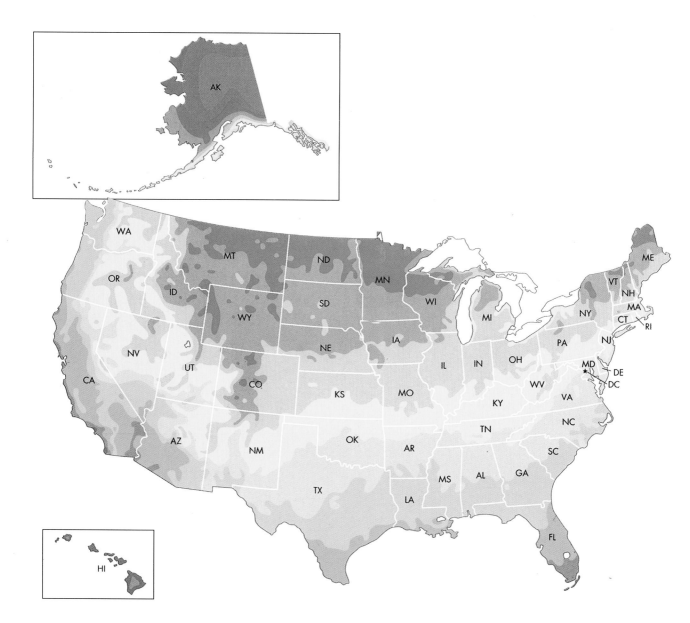

This hardiness zone system developed by the United States Department of Agriculture is based on the average annual minimum temperatures for each zone. All plants in the A–Z of Grasses (pages 21–85) are rated with a zone indicating the coldest temperatures they will reliably survive and perform consistently. The plant may also be grown in all zones warmer than the one indicated. However, the zone system is only a guide. Microclimates within each zone may mean you can grow plants from a warmer zone, or conversely, some plants hardy to your zone may not survive in your garden. This is particularly true toward the upper and lower limits of each zone. Gardeners living outside the USA can deduce the zone in which they live based on their own average minimum temperature.

	Fahrenheit	Celsius
Zone 1	below -50°	below -46°
Zone 2	-50° to -40°	-46° to -40°
Zone 3	-40° to -30°	-40° to -34°
Zone 4	-30° to -20°	-34° to -29°
Zone 5	-20° to -10°	-29° to -23°
Zone 6	-10° to 0°	-23° to -18°
Zone 7	0° to 10°	-18° to -12°
Zone 8	10° to 20°	-12° to -7°
Zone 9	20° to 30°	-7° to -1°
Zone 10	30° to 40°	-1° to 4°
Zone 11	above 40°	above 4°

Index